RED BALL IN THE SKY

Red Ball in the Sky

CHARLES F. BLAIR

Foreword by Lowell Thomas

JARROLDS, LONDON

JARROLDS PUBLISHERS (LONDON) LTD
178–202 Great Portland Street, London W1

AN IMPRINT OF THE HUTCHINSON GROUP

London Melbourne Sydney Auckland
Johannesburg Cape Town

First published 1970

Printed in Great Britain by litho on antique wove paper
by Anchor Press, and bound by Wm. Brendon,
both of Tiptree, Essex
ISBN 0 09 103910 X

To Maureen

To Fran [illegible]

May you enjoy this. you [illegible].

Keep [illegible] flying.

Darling.

xxxxxxxx

Foreword

by Lowell Thomas

To all who are, or who are likely to be, concerned:

This is to tell you a little about Charles F. Blair—flyer by compulsion, writer by instinct, and now provocateur by design.

We are all acquainted with the credentials necessary to flyers and writers, but how does one qualify as a provocateur? The answer is as near as the nearest dictionary, which defines the word as "one who serves or tends to provoke, stimulate or incense." For having written this book, Charlie Blair is just such a man.

Red Ball in the Sky is essentially an action story—for the most part, a colorful, often thrilling, always engrossing account of the life and times of one of America's great pilots. As such, it tells of his rousing adventures from fledgling naval aviator to trail-blazing civilian pilot and all the way to Air Force general in a modern military "think factory." And here, too, are the feats to earn him the prestigious Harmon International Trophy (for the first solo flight across the Arctic Ocean and the North Pole), the Thurlow Award (for "outstanding contribution to the science of navigation") and the Distinguished Flying Cross (for heading the first flight of jet fighters across the North Pole). All of which should serve as a comfort, incidentally, to those who currently travel with him as a senior captain on Pan Am's round-the-world jet routes.

However, *Red Ball in the Sky* is far more than a fascinating narrative. It contains the analytical reflections of a technician who is knowledgeably aware of the awesome problems generated by the uncontrolled proliferation of thermonuclear weapons, and who knows and respects America's mighty deterrent power; a man who is, nevertheless, willing—indeed, champing at the bit—to help dispel the myths and shibboleths of America's present policy for defense against nuclear attack. He is a man, above all, who raises questions that must be answered if the United States is to survive nuclear confrontation on a global scale.

Contents

Illustrations

Cast of Characters

EXCALIBUR I — A four-engine Sikorsky VS-44 flying boat, and the first airliner to fly passengers and mail nonstop across the North Atlantic. This magnificent airplane came to an untimely end; during an attempted takeoff at Botwood, Newfoundland, it went to the bottom of the Bay of Exploits.

EXCALIBUR II — A twin-engine Curtiss C-46 Commando. This big transport circulated among five continents as a tramp airliner until it met its demise on a ridge of the Andes near La Paz.

EXCALIBUR III — A single-engine, single-seat P-51 Mustang fighter built by North American Aviation. This long-legged fighter held the transatlantic speed record and was the first airplane to be flown solo across the Arctic and the North Pole. It survived all its adventures and found final hangar space at the Smithsonian's National Air Museum in Washington.

EXCALIBUR IV A single-engine, single-seat F84-F jet fighter built by Republic Aviation. It served adventurously as an airborne navigational laboratory, but like many a great soldier it was retired and left to rust away in a boneyard for unwanted airplanes.

EXCALIBUR V A single-engine, two-place F100-F Supersabre fighter built by North American Aviation. It was the lead aircraft of the first flight of jet fighters to cross the Arctic Ocean and the North Pole. Its final destination was our Far East Air Force in Asia, where it became a casualty of the war in Vietnam.

EXCALIBUR VI A Republic F-105D single-engine, single seat fighter which was the first of several jet fighters I coaxed faster than twice the speed of sound. This airplane made its last flight out of Thailand, and its remains lie on Thud Ridge near the outskirts of Hanoi.

I was the pilot who flew these *Excaliburs*. I was lucky enough not to be aboard their final flights, except that of *Excalibur III* when it was delivered to the National Air Museum.

—*Charles F. Blair*

PART I

Arctic Solo

EXCALIBUR III's POLAR FLIGHT

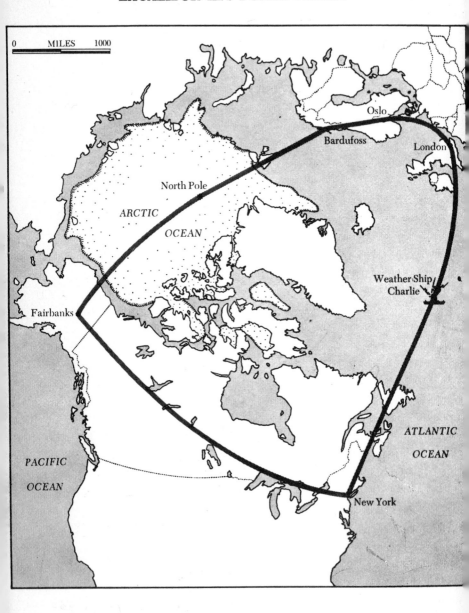

CHAPTER ONE

Chocks Away

Every move is with an eye on the clock. I look upward through the cockpit canopy at the snow-flecked granite along the canyon's north rim. Within minutes I will scale those jagged cliffs and take leave of Norway.

Over the nose of my single-engine P-51 fighter a mile of runway splits the steep pine forest of Bardufoss fjord. Mechanically I go through the departure check list, casting an eye on levers, switches, and instruments. Everything is ready.

Lieutenant Gaarde of the Norwegian Royal Air Force stands at *Excalibur III*'s wing tip, his face grim with concern. He points anxiously at a small rivulet of gasoline which is coursing along the undersurface of the wing. But I give him a thumbs up. I've had long experience with this chronic leak which occurs whenever the wing is brimful of fuel from wing tip to wing tip. I know the rate of leakage and it's not serious. It will stop flowing when the fuel in the outer wing panels has been partly used up.

The minute hand of the clock is creeping up on the 1500 Greenwich Mean Time deadline for takeoff, and I must not be late. Because the ordinary magnetic compass will be useless in the far north, my little ship will be guided only by the sun. The sun angles measured around the horizon won't fit the flight plan if I run too many minutes late, and a landfall on the coast of Siberia could do worse than jolt my navigational ego. It might spoil the trip.

But today, May 29, 1951, I'm not thinking of losing. Beyond the north rim of the fjord is the beckoning Arctic —an ocean that has never been flown solo, and my route to Fairbanks in Alaska, thirty-three hundred miles away, has an extra feature. It lies directly across the North Pole.

I've had moments of doubt. My enthusiasm for this enterprise has risen, or ebbed, depending on whom I've seen and talked with. It plunged close to rock bottom the other day, when a Pan Am pilot colleague from back home made his scheduled stop at Oslo's Gardemoen Airport flying the kind of airplane I was most accustomed to—a big airliner, supported by four engines. My friend found me flat on my back on the hangar concrete helping a mechanic wrestle with the P-51's corroded tail-wheel strut, a detail which threatened to rupture the tail-wheel tire whenever I overloaded the airplane.

Like many of my American friends who have considered this flight to be foolhardy, he was solemnly sympathetic about the possibilities, but he couldn't hide the impression of being certain this was the last he would see of me. I was acutely depressed by his graveside manner, and was temporarily struck with an urge to scuttle this lonely expedition and hustle back to my sane flying job in charge of a Pan Am Stratocruiser. Only a man "touched in the head" could spend his vacation this way, working on his tomb.

But my recently acquired Norwegian friends, besides being less personally concerned, are also more attuned to the Arctic. The far north is part of *their* domain. They have so rekindled my spirit that today, with all the troublesome details of preparation finally overcome, my zest for adventure rose with the sun when it came out of the forest east of Gardemoen.

But what, deep down at the bottom of a supposedly sane psyche, ever brought me to Bardufoss in the first place? What could cause a forty-one-year-old New Yorker, secure and well paid in a stimulating airline assignment, with twenty years of professional flying to back up his judgment, to bring an overloaded P-51 fighter to such a remote fjord in the far north of Norway?

The fact that I was already deeply involved with this high-performance airplane certainly had something to do with it. This retired, though still youthful war-horse has a new, overloaded fuel capacity which I redesigned into its wings and fuselage, and I also added a sixteen-hour supply of oxygen. It's now capable of stretching its speedy legs more than four thousand nonstop miles. Who could resist climbing into such a phenomenal flying machine and exploring some faraway place?

Curiosity could be another reason. During millions of miles of flying I've never seen the North Pole. My curiosity is insatiable.

Money sometimes beckons a man to stick his neck out, but this consideration, I can honestly say, is not compelling today. There is no bag of gold dangling in Alaska, no visible money anywhere, except that I'm hopeful that Pan American Airways, like a benevolent parent, will pick up the fuel bill.

The prospect of acclaim is sometimes dazzling to the

uninitiated, but I've been around long enough to be wary of it. Moreover, the difference between heroics and foolishness is often razor-thin. I'm no longer a youngster seeking a quick breakthrough to fame in the wild blue yonder. Instead, my reputation as a professional aviator will certainly suffer if this journey is anything but a total success. It would take only a minute arithmetical mistake, a momentary lapse of flying judgment, a straying of concentration, or the failure of one of many thousands of moving metal parts that make up the engine and its accessories to brand me a fool—and a dead one, at that.

There is another, harder-to-explain reason for my coming here. It seemed altogether minor when it happened. In fact, it was only a casual conversation that finally catalyzed this smallest of all polar expeditions. Although I was springloaded to go, anyway, it took an extra nudge to get off dead center.

This extra shove came from a pair of Air Force navigators who were too cocksure and patronizing about what they had been doing in the Arctic. They had been navigating big airplanes up there, and had by now hung a NO TRESPASSING sign on *their* North Pole. No single-seaters allowed, they seemed to say when they suggested that a solo flight across the top of the world was too impractical to even discuss.

I got the impression these two mortals were among a select few who navigationally owned the Arctic Ocean. One of them staked his claim with this admonishment: "You can't fly alone in the polar regions. Our Arctic B-29s each carry three navigators and a half ton of navigation equipment. The Arctic, my friend, is no piece of cake."

I could feel my temperature rise. My combative instincts were so stirred that failing to accept the challenge would have been intolerable. Here was a myth that needed deflating.

I developed a scheme for pricking this Arctic balloon by boiling down flight procedures to the simplest routine and by figuring out a way of doing the complicated navigation work beforehand—prepackaged navigation. First, I worked out an easygoing, foolproof celestial navigation technique based on ten years of practice over the Atlantic. Those years of eyeballing the sun and star angles through fleeting breaks in the overcast had given me a flair for devising celestial procedures that even a moron could manage.

Next, I had to make sure my celestial equipment would fit within some stingy limitations. It would need to be simple and easy to operate. It also had to be inexpensive, small in size, and light of weight. Therefore the whole package has been boiled down to a total of one sun compass, one bubble sextant, and *three* watches. I'll take no chances with the time of day.

Simplicity is the key requirement. My working quarters are cramped, and along with accelerating fatigue will come the intellect-depressing effects of ten hours of high-altitude flight in an unpressurized cockpit, subsisting on oxygen in the deadly thin air.

But celestial navigation isn't the only problem confronting me. There are other aspects of this journey which do not respond to such predigested treatment.

This takeoff is one of them.

The runway strip ahead is surrounded by lofty mountains with only one opening—to the east. The easterly takeoff will be stretched by a tantalizing tailwind, and my airplane is overloaded so far beyond design limits that it rides too heavily on its troublesome tail wheel. If the tailwind freshens without warning, or if the corroded tail wheel collapses after I've used up too much concrete, my fuel-glutted craft could suddenly turn into a billow of black smoke at the far end of the runway.

This is my own airplane, bought with my own hard-flown cash—in fact, everything I had in the bank. I'm shooting the works on this sunny spring day above the Arctic Circle.

Lieutenant Gaarde raises his hand and points at his wrist watch. My hand goes to the throttle.

At 1458 the chocks are away.

For twenty-three years, ever since I first flew solo in 1928, I have been preparing for this adventure, but I was unaware until last summer exactly where or when it would take place. Flying fighters in the Navy and at Grumman; hundreds of Atlantic crossings in airliners; and even further back, years of scraping across the Continental Divide with the pioneers of the Air Mail have made me as ready as anyone can be for taking on the Arctic.

The men of the Air Mail never knew it, but they had a share in my Arctic experience. A man is often conditioned by the company he keeps, especially when he is inclined the same way, and some of the mail pioneers' zest for adventure may have rubbed off on me when we flew in the same cockpit together.

Earlier this morning I flew from Oslo northward to my Arctic takeoff strip at Bardufoss. As I swept across Norway's spectacular interlace of snow-capped mountains and deeply fissured valleys, my thoughts roamed back almost a score of years to other mountains—to the great Rockies of my own country, and to the days when my first inclination toward flying a fast airplane into the far reaches of the world was a long way short of reality.

At that time I was flying the mountain run west of Cheyenne, a Union Pacific railroad town on the edge of the Wyoming prairie near where the Rocky Mountains begin. In 1933 Cheyenne was also the headquarters of Boeing Air Transport, the Chicago–San Francisco segment of

United Air Lines* which was Air Mail Route Number One, America's first transcontinental airway, better known to the men of the Air Mail as AM-1.

I had joined up with Boeing Air Transport on one of Cheyenne's soft and sunny June days, and was scheduled to fly as copilot the following evening. I knew very little about the airplane I was assigned to—the new Boeing 247 —except for one thing. Someone had taught me how to raise and lower the landing gear, a new feature on the airlines. This was the only mechanical complexity. There were no flaps or other aerodynamic trimmings on the 247.

I was told my flight would be Trip Three, the night transcontinental, departing shortly before midnight. I would fly the Cheyenne–Salt Lake City sector. The pilot would be Mr. Henry Boonstra.

I was glad to get the mountain run. It was more sporting to fly among the hills than over the prairie.

It was late evening when Boonstra arrived at the airport. He was fresh from the Buzzard's Roost, otherwise known as the Plaza Hotel, where the pilots of the transcontinental took their ease and waited for their airplanes, killing time with high stake poker, rummy, or chess.

Henry Boonstra was one of the intellectuals whose specialty was chess. Having made his presence known he wasted no time with unnecessary chatter. I found him hunched over a tiny portable chessboard in the far corner of the dispatch office, a place where pilots gathered to swap anecdotes with the ground staff before pushing off into the Wyoming sky. There was no flight plan to fuss with. This formality had not yet been devised.

While waiting for Trip Three to come in from the

---

* United Air Lines in 1933 was a loose amalgamation of four airlines: National Air Transport, the eastern segment, covered the New York–Chicago–Dallas route; Boeing Air Transport operated from Chicago west to San Francisco; Pacific Air Transport flew the West Coast from Seattle to San Diego; Varney Air Lines had the Pacific Northwest route from Portland, Oregon, to Salt Lake City.

prairie, Mr. Boonstra cagily contemplated the disposition of his knights, bishops, and rooks which were engaged in a complex assault on his opponent's king. Being thus pre-occupied his greeting was perfunctory, but his smile was pleasant.

His well-worn uniform was of forest green, resembling that of a Western Union messenger boy. But Henry Boonstra lent stature to any uniform, with or without insignia. There were no brass buttons, or any indication of rank other than the gold wings of graceful design embossed with the inscription U.S. Air Mail. My own wings, when I got them, would be identical, except that the word "Mate" would be bolted conspicuously on top, making clear who was in charge, and effectively separating the men from the boys. It would be three years before I shed this humble tag and experienced the heady exuberance that goes with a pilot's first airline command.

My enthusiasm for this nocturnal undertaking quickened at first contact with this mountain pilot. His friendly smile advertised a modest and uncomplicated disposition. Some pilots merely waggled their jowls with a grudging grunt, thus indicating the presence of a copilot to be barely tolerable.

Though only in his forties, Henry Boonstra was the sage of the mountain run. The rocks and ridges, desert and forest between Cheyenne and Salt Lake City have been his specialty since the earliest days of the transcontinental air mail. As part of the air-mail legend Boonstra commanded the kind of respect that was more like awe in a new copilot.

Years of lonely combat with the elements in single-engine mail planes were reflected in the lines of a face that was extra strong along the chin line, an impression accentuated by the weathering of sun and slipstream. Although his hair was approaching white, it was unlikely that nervous stress and strain had much to do with its pigmentation. In Boonstra there was no trace of the worry wart. He had no shortage of inner resources.

I inquired if there were any special instructions. His reply was diffident, as if he hadn't become accustomed to flying with an assistant. Any formal briefing would have been totally unnatural.

The chess game was put away after duly recording its status. We moved out onto the tarmac to find a twin-engine monoplane in the glare of the brightly lit terminal. It disgorged a small assortment of intrepid passengers, followed by the crewmen who had guided it uphill from Omaha. The pilot was Rube Wagner, a man cast from a mold very much like Boonstra's.

By day or night I would find the Boonstra cockpit demeanor to be as gentle and unabashed as his earthbound personality, although this did not hold true for all pilots. An affable Doctor Jekyll on the ground could quickly become a ferocious Mr. Hyde at the gentlest bruising of a swollen ego, or a slight rise of cockpit pressure.

Under heavy adversity Mr. Boonstra could be guilty of a vexed "Gee whiz." Under maximum pressure the invective became a gentle "Rats." His mannerisms of movement were always smooth and deliberate. There was never any fearful and disorderly darting of hands. I found that even the manner of throwing a switch could reveal much about a man's disposition and state of mind.

On this cloudless June night we pushed westward into Laramie Valley, flying at nine thousand feet on the altimeter which cleared Sherman Hill by a couple of hundred feet—a lot of clearance to a mountain pilot. The Sherman Hill beacon gave a reassuring blink as we skimmed by, flashing a light on the cockpit instruments.

"Stay at nine thousand and two-eighty on the compass," Mr. Boonstra purred gently, indicating I should take over the controls. "After Elk Mountain just follow the lights." He rested his head against the side window and appeared to settle down for a nap. It was past midnight and any sensible fellow should be sleeping.

I hoped he was faking. He was surely aware this was my first flight across the mountains. Although his right eye was closed, the other would certainly be cagily open. We were flying below the level of nearby hills in a blackness that was total, and I was not altogether sure about the whereabouts of Elk Mountain.

I was getting the heat treatment and had to show my hand. Undoubtedly Mr. Boonstra was playing a game, probing for a display of anxiety that would expose an undisciplined nervous system. He was curious if I would do what I was told without unseemly loquacity or other neurotic display, such as letting the altimeter creep up to an altitude that didn't suit him. He was probably wondering, too, if this newly hired copilot could fly well enough to hold altitude and compass heading at night.

I kept my mouth shut and flew at nine thousand on a 280 degree heading exactly as told. We were skimming close to the ridge of Medicine Bow Forest with no trace of a ground light that could offer any guidance. The only man-made lights that marred the purity of this Wyoming night were faint pinpricks from beacons on the airway curving far to the north through the metropolis of Medicine Bow. But those distant beacons off the starboard wing merely popped into occasional view on the horizon like intermittent stars of stealthy disposition.

The night was moonless, with a faint shimmer of light from countless stars and the Milky Way. A star in the west helped with the steering and I resolved to settle any doubts that might lurk in the head of my curious companion.

I found that the nearness of the unseen forest fascinated me and gave me an odd sense of well-being—a thirst for danger not entirely abnormal in youthful aviators.

As we skirted the north fringe of the forest, I felt the urge to flash some light on the tall pines below for no reason other than to investigate the efficiency of the landing lights. But I hesitated to reach across the cockpit and brashly desecrate the darkness. Although Mr. Boonstra appeared to be sleeping, I was certain he was sizing me up. To flash the lights would be bad manners, casting doubt on the altitude he had selected to fly.

The cockpit lights were so dim that I became aware of the shapeless black mass of the forest which rose to twelve thousand feet not far to the south on a granite battlement called Snowy Range. But the forest ahead appeared to be dropping away—which would signal our approach to the pass which separates Medicine Bow Forest from Elk Mountain.

The air was smooth; we seemed to hang motionless. The airspeed was pegged at a hundred and forty-five and the propellers flailed noisily. A towering black shadow separated itself from the shapeless mass below, where Elk Mountain should have been if we were still on course.

The tall mass loomed close, and suddenly a beacon flashed over the nose as we crossed the north ridge to spring clear of the mountain. We had escaped the threatening shadow and shaken off the fascination of the forest. From here the airway bent twenty degrees left toward a long string of airway beacons twinkling like fireflies in a desert that stretched all the way to the beginnings of Utah.

Elk Mountain, where the airway bends, was astern. In the previous century the Overland Trail wound through a pass in the mountain's north flank. Its trace could still be seen in daytime by anyone flying close to the terrain.

At night Elk Mountain was just a huge shadow. By day it was a real hunk of mountain, jutting from the northwest extremity of Medicine Bow Forest like an overly prominent chin. Its steep slopes were heavily whiskered with ever-green which degenerated to a sparse unkempt stubble on top.

To a mountain pilot each mountain had its special personality. Elk Mountain was clearly a villain, having proven this point to the next of kin of many an aviator and passenger. It was a sly mountain because its untidy summit poked a couple of hundred feet above eleven thousand. Had its balding pate grown a few hundred feet shorter, this hostile outcropping would have collected fewer victims. Pilots who were too fastidious about flying a precise eleven thousand on their altimeters, and who were disorderly navigators, had gone to their reward at this popular eastbound altitude.

But the undertaker at Medicine Bow never complained.

Henry Boonstra roused himself from his pretended slumber when we swung past Elk Mountain toward the long line of flashing desert beacons. "Drop down to eight thousand," he advised, aware, I hoped, that the small needle of the altimeter hadn't budged off the number nine. His manner was less reserved, suggesting my stock had risen a few points during the past thirty minutes.

Passing the first mountain test gave me a sense of well-being. Flying jobs were hard to find in this depression year 1933, especially with a big-league airline, and it took some hard chasing to get this one. Cast loose from the Pacific Fleet because the Navy was too broke to extend further active duty to its reservists, I had hurried off to Cheyenne only a week ago on a quest for this copilot's seat I now occupied.

At Cheyenne that day I found Boeing Air Transport's chief pilot, H.T. "Slim" Lewis, crawling out from under a tall stack of job applications from which he would sort out a handful of copilots for his new Boeing 247s. Some sixty of these sleek, ten-passenger, one-hundred-and-seventy-mile-an-hour airliners were on order for United Air Lines, and Mr. Lewis would get his share. These airplanes would begin a revolution in air transport.

Shoving aside the offending stack of applications, Mr. Lewis grunted testily, "Not a chance." He regarded me suspiciously, like a fellow sampling ripe cheese, while we chatted about the merits of Army versus Navy pilots. I became aware he preferred landlubbers.

The interview seemed totally negative. Even my sanity was questioned for traveling all the way from San Diego in pursuit of a goal clearly beyond reach.

There had been plenty of forewarning. My self-extolling telegram of a few days before, heavily larded with self-alleged aviation virtue, somehow hadn't rocked this segment of the air-transport industry. The curt return wire, collect, from this same Mr. Lewis had carried the touch of an icicle: "Retel, no openings."

So what was a naval aviator doing in Cheyenne, face-to-face with this granite-faced veteran of the Air Mail? Seven hundred flying hours, much of it over the ocean, was insignificant to the old pros who flew a thousand hours a year over mountain and prairie. Any hope of joining the Air Mail elite had certainly glimmered away, and it was a long way back to blue water.

Thoughts of the deep blue sea brought a new surge of optimism and sent me hurrying east in search of a flying job with Pan American Airways, a young airline which was operating flying boats in the Caribbean. The dream of most Navy pilots not intent on a naval career was to fly for this expanding company.

Logic, too, suggested that seagoing pilots stick to their flying boats, and I had long since set my sights on Pan Am, even before entering the Navy flying school at Pensacola.

But a message from the frosty Slim Lewis caught up

with me in Chicago, and halted my ocean-flying ambitions. He offered that copilot's seat in the new Boeing, and a bird in the hand in the year 1933 was better than any dream.

When Pan Am's flying offer came my way not long afterward it wasn't easy to stay on dry land in Cheyenne. But it was a lucky decision to stay awhile in the mountains and fly elbow to elbow with the great men of the Air Mail. These descendants of the Pony Express showed me how airplanes should, and should not, be flown, and in all kinds of weather. It was a rugged education. Pan Am would come later, by way of an airline merger.

From Elk Mountain the Wyoming desert stretches two hundred miles to its western extremity on the Utah state boundary where the heavily forested Uinta and Wasatch ranges start cluttering the airway again. Ridges and buttes abound in the desert, but these were less exacting obstructions than the big mountains.

A blond young lady opened the cockpit door behind me to give a warm smile and an offering of coffee. She was a pretty creature in spite of a voluminous uniform which did anything but justice to what it contained. It wasn't like this in the Navy and appeared to be a good feature. In 1933 a stewardess was of a species as rare as a buffalo, and the small group of intrepid young women who flew for Boeing Air Transport had more to offer than just a smile. They were all registered nurses, able to doctor the less hardy travelers.

At eight thousand feet we skimmed across an inconspicuous ridge that marked the Continental Divide. The emergency field at Parco was behind us. The next chance for an emergency landing would be a flat spot on the desert called Cherokee, situated alongside the Union Pacific railroad and Lincoln Highway. If an engine failed we couldn't hold our altitude in spite of the claims in the airplane manufacturer's brochure. The remaining engine could only stretch the glide in the thin air of the Rocky Mountains. But that was good enough for Henry Boonstra. Two engines were a luxury after so many years with only one. During those years a forced landing, even a crash, was just part of the day's work.

We eased past Cherokee, which automatically blinked a friendly green light beneath its rotating beacon. Cherokee's lone caretaker was undoubtedly snatching some sleep in his little white shack. Our engines were droning smoothly, so there would be no need to disturb him, but there would be times when this small patch of flat desert could look like the Garden of Eden.

These emergency airfields averaged some forty miles from one another, and there were a total of nine between Cheyenne and Salt Lake City. The fields at Cherokee, Bitter Creek, and Knight were Wyoming outposts with a population of one. The other fields were more sociably situated near a town or village.

Visits at these desert airfields became more frequent when the winter weather clamped down on the airway. A cluster of five-gallon fuel tins was usually available to succor a thirsty airplane. The half-frozen copilot poured gasoline into the slippery wings while the pilot toasted himself over the stove in the caretaker's shack, quizzing its lonely proprietor on the prospects of bagging an antelope when the next hunting season rolled around.

Mr. Boonstra broke his silence to give Trip Three's radio report as the lights of Rock Springs passed by the starboard wing. There was no wastage of words.

"Salt Lake from Trip Three. We're ten south of Rock Springs."

Salt Lake answered back through a crackle and bang of ear-shattering static. I wondered if Mr. Boonstra, having roused himself, would be taking over the controls. But he just settled back again as if altogether detached from the proceedings.

Green River went by and the cockpit finally came alive with the first dialogue since Elk Mountain. Mr. Boonstra's new orders, as always, were polite and precise.

"Steer two thirty and fly at seventy-five hundred."

"Yes, sir." I was still at the controls and beginning to feel pretty sure of myself.

We trespassed a stretch of badlands, a place where nothing much grows, not even the rugged sage or the tumbling tumbleweed. The airway beacons dwindled away to the north toward Granger. Once again the night became totally black.

Our new cruising altitude would surely clear everything in front of us, but I suspected we were at the very bottom of this big Wyoming sky. Mr. Boonstra was indeed playing cagey with the headwinds, and he certainly showed great faith in the reliability of those impersonal little needles on the altimeter. In due course I would become equally convinced, after years of skimming low across the mountains and desert.

We were getting close to the tall Uintas which towered above thirteen thousand feet along the south flank of the airway. By this time I was feeling increasingly grandiose about doing all the flying. After a few more trips I wouldn't need Mr. Boonstra.

We rejoined the airway beacons again at the beginning of a vast clutter of mountains. "Climb to nine thousand" was the next terse command.

Nine thousand would clear the south ridge of Porcupine by a conservative three hundred feet. I was still at the controls and was now almost sure Mr. Boonstra intended to let me take it all the way.

I knew nothing about the Salt Lake City airport or its approaches, and had never seen a Boeing 247 being landed from the vantage point of the cockpit, not even in daylight. The thought of making my first airline landing at night, on my first trip, and with passengers, added enough extra adrenalin to alert all faculties. Thus stimulated I made ready to show how it was done in the Navy.

My exhilaration was short-lived. Twenty miles from Salt Lake City, at the moment I had planned to begin *my* descent, Mr. Boonstra smiled graciously and grasped the controls.

The wind went out of my sails. Suddenly deflated, I settled back to see how the old pro would do it.

The high ridges of the Wasatch were silhouetted against a glow of lights from the city beyond. Ahead of us, carved into this formidable mountain barrier, was a flyable canyon called Emigration.

Mr. Boonstra—I could never be brash enough to call him Henry—poked the airplane's nose down toward the canyon's black bottom and went hellbent for the lights along Salt Lake City's eastern rim.

We landed with a flourish, without wasting a second on the clock. I was beginning to learn.

When the clouds hung low on the mountains and the visibility underneath was near zero in snow, it was fascinating to behold the mountain mail men display their own individual methods for getting the mail through. One of the more exacting techniques at night called for circling a canyon beacon below the level of nearby peaks, waiting for the snow squall ahead to move past the next beacon. On these occasions the slowest freight train on the Union Pacific showed us its heels.

I discovered that almost any kind of weather could be flown successfully if the pilot took the trouble to work out the details in advance. Bob Bergesen, one of the more scientific pilots, was especially adept at outthinking the elements, and gave an unforgettable demonstration at Rock Springs on a blizzardy winter night.

Rock Springs Airport in those days was a small patch of dirt carved out of the desert, and was closely hemmed in by two parallel ridges known as Gunn Mountain and White Mountain. The visibility on this night was near zero in heavy snow, and we were scheduled to exercise our favorite fueling hose at this Wyoming outpost, or else flop down at some less exalted airport to wrestle with a collection of five-gallon tins.

Bergesen pivoted around the barely visible airport beacon a thousand feet above the hangar roof, shortening his radius of turn by flying close to a stall at eighty miles an hour. Being on the ragged edge of safe flying speed, the wing now and then shuddered its protest when dipped too steeply, but these minor stall warnings were just part of the technique, and a convenient reminder to level the wings a little.

This mixture of visual and instrument flying kept Bergesen's eyes roving between the almost invisible beacon below his open side window and the cockpit instruments by which he made certain the airplane was still right side up. Eventually the snow slackened, brightening the flash of the airport beacon just enough to satisfy Bergesen's educated instinct. Then down we went, picking up speed in a steep spiral to pounce on the snow-smitten airport like a starving pelican diving for minnow.

The pilot who radiated the most zest for adventure was Jack Knight, and the fact that this great pilot was a man apart was quickly revealed to a new copilot in the intimate confines of an airplane cockpit. He flew with supreme confidence, yet without any trace of bravado. He possessed the right blend of audacity and caution which, with luck, permits a pilot to fly boldly and still grow old.

This remarkable aviator was no matinée idol to look at,

being a little on the frail side with a tendency toward five o'clock shadow, but he was a giant in the history of the transcontinental. He was the first to fly the mails at night, and his exploits over the Rockies and Great Plains were legendary among the men of the Air Mail. It was Knight's flying credo, like that of Charles Lindbergh, which had much to do with my coming to Bardufoss fjord in the far north of Norway.

The man who possessed seniority number one among air-mail pilots was E. Hamilton Lee, whose normal route was between Omaha and Cheyenne. One of Lee's unforgettable habits, when hard pressed, was his custom of opening the cockpit side window when the visibility was low, and sticking his head out, hoping to see better. It was quite a sight—this pint-size aviator, with his head projected into the wintry blasts, the uniform cap reversed with the visor pointing aft, a mangled cigar tightly clamped to starboard of a tiny mustache and angled sharply inboard for protection against the windstream. In the winter this open-cockpit technique froze his copilot to the hardness of stone, rendering him reasonably harmless.

Normally, this cagey airman flew a cautious, rather than bold, airplane. His reputation needed no further embellishment. It was only when the younger generation impolitely tried to outfly him that the window flew open and the cap was reversed. When deeply prodded he would fly "under the weather" when the cloud ceiling was reported near zero. On one occasion on a misty morning saturated with rain and fog, we flew along the valley of the Missouri from the northwest, skimming only a few feet above the muddy waters, weaving with the bends of the river, easing up over clumps of trees, skirting steep bluffs that loomed dimly a few yards from the wing tip. Suddenly the edge of the airport popped into view and we touched down. I felt like kissing the tarmac. No one else landed in Omaha that day.

The pilot who could fly as low as anyone could go and still stay airborne was Werner Bunge. My first daylight westbound flight out of Cheyenne was a gopher's-eye view of Wyoming's rust-colored wasteland. While crossing Red Desert, a Union Pacific trainman gave us the eye from the cupola of his caboose. He looked down at us—not up—as we cruised by.

But this stocky, bristle-headed Teuton was also most considerate of his passengers. To put their minds at ease he would go aft among them with his violin to give his own special interpretation of Bach and Beethoven, leaving the copilot alone to skim low across the sage.

When I joined up with Boeing, there were ten of these mountain men who regularly flew as command pilots on the Cheyenne–Salt Lake run. Within the space of a few years 50 percent of the pilots—Hal Collison, Tommy Thompson, Julius Barr, Jack Rose, and Lloyd Anderson—ran out of luck, although not all of them came to grief in the mountains. The remaining five had better fortune, but they, too, were the apple of every undertaker's eye, as were the copilots who flew with them.

Anderson was the first to go, straight down into Parley's Summit, near Salt Lake, in a January 1934 snowstorm. Collison would be next.

Hal Collison ranked with Henry Boonstra as a pioneer of the mountain mail. He was a big, tough-talking fellow with a none-too-gentle visage and a reputation for being stern with copilots. However, after a couple of years and a large number of trips together, Colly and I had achieved a good level of harmony in the cockpit. In the beginning it wasn't easy, but eventually the mountain tough guy had become downright affable. Perhaps he had reached the conclusion that copilots weren't altogether useless, especially when he practiced his instrument flying. Lately he had buckled down to learn more about this new aspect of his job.

On our last flight together we climbed aboard **Trip Four** on a balmy, moonless, Salt Lake midnight, and soon our eastbound transcontinental was poking its nose up through Emigration Canyon. Colly leveled off at ten thousand feet and then dropped his seat near the floor where he could see only the little round dials in front of him. Then he turned the white lights on the panel up as bright as they would go and started flying by instruments.

I pondered the possibility that this old-timer among mountain men wasn't really happy with his eyes riveted to those demanding little gauges. He surely mourned the day when seat-of-the-pants skill was the key to survival on this run across the Continental Divide. Nowadays lesser men were trespassing his once exclusive domain, and they were full of new methods, plus the chill of big-time efficiency.

The airline no longer needed skillful dead-stick landings in the mountains and desert with an engine gone sour. By the year 1935 the engines of the 247 had become more comfortably reliable, and they had recently been beefed up, so that the airplane could actually fly on one engine. Therefore it was not likely that Colly could further embellish his well-decorated escutcheon, which included more than twenty dead-stick landings between Cheyenne and Salt Lake City.

The last time he did it was in a tri-motor Boeing biplane with a load of passengers and mail. Somehow all three engines quit at the same time. Afterward someone irreverently suggested that the old maestro had brushed his heavy winter flying suit against the master ignition switch while squeezing back into his seat after a long chitchat with the passengers in the cabin.

No damage was done, although the landing was at nine thousand feet above sea level in deep snow on the high ridge of Porcupine, completely without help from any of those unsympathetic engines. Having put the plane there,

Colly was told to fly it out, which he did after the winter slackened and a crew of lumberjacks hacked out a longer clearing.

But the night after my last flight with Colly the old-timer's luck would change.

I was close at hand, westbound out of Cheyenne. We were taxiing out for takeoff when a familiar voice rang loud and clear in the early morning stillness, "Trip Four over Silver Crown."

It was Colly. He was eastbound from Salt Lake again, and tonight his copilot happened to be a stranger, a lad borrowed from the flatlands east of Cheyenne.

The Cheyenne radio operator spieled off the ground wind and setting of the altimeter, but there was no reply from the eastbound transcontinental. The sky in the west was suddenly totally quiet.

We took off into the night sky and headed west toward the beacon light at Silver Crown. The night was cloudless and so clear that the distant beacon atop Sherman Hill sparkled like a brightly lit diamond. We flashed our landing lights and stared hard into the west for Colly's answering blink. But we looked in vain, and all the while the urgent wail of the Cheyenne radio operator probed the night, assailing our eardrums with a dirge of landing instructions.

But the old man of the mountains couldn't hear. He was down on the rolling prairie with all hands, and they wouldn't be flying again. He had conquered the big mountains once more, only to have the gentle ridge at Silver Crown reach up and take him.

There was no fire—not even a spark. We cruised overhead without knowing.

CHAPTER TWO

Aldebaran's Warning

The first requisite for navigating in the Arctic with assurance and precision is to know the traveling habits and timetable of the stars, sun, planets, and moon.

It took many years of celestial practice to gather the confidence I took along in my P-51 to Bardufoss. I had originally become enamored with these heavenly wonders while flying the mountains of Wyoming. Then, in the war years, we put them to work in the sky over the North Atlantic. In fact, during those uncertain days there was little else to navigate by, and oftentimes we had to be satisfied with only a fleeting glimpse of an occasional star over a span of thousands of nonstop miles.

Nowadays, by contrast, we streak across the Atlantic in our high-flying jets guided by electronic devices, and pay little heed to our celestial friends of bygone years.

Our forsaken comrades in the heavens above have become as remote and impersonal as the ocean below.

But it wasn't always high and fast on the Atlantic. There were times when we flew our flying boats so low that the windshields were spattered with salt spray, and a flight across the Atlantic with several fuel stops often took days instead of hours.

Moreover, during those war years, the targets we had to shoot at—a few friendly harbors in Britain, Ireland, and Portugal—offered only faint and spurious radio signals to assist a bad-weather landfall. Nor could the consequences of a mistaken landfall be taken lightly. Most of Europe lay under the control of the enemy.

It was under these demanding conditions that celestial navigation became second nature to me, so much so that the navigation problems linked to flying in the polar regions would eventually become a tantalizing challenge.

I first learned to shoot the stars and sun in the backyard of my home in Cheyenne. In 1936, after exchanging a month's pay for an aircraft bubble sextant, I raised a few eyebrows by introducing celestial navigation to the transcontinental airway.

One thing led to another, and in 1940 I found myself installed in the boss pilot's chair of a new overseas airline that would give Pan American Airways such a run for its transatlantic money that within ten years it would become a leading carrier on the North Atlantic. At this point it was sold and became part of Pan Am.

Flying a desk wasn't altogether a pleasure for an aviator whose place of business the past seven years had been the transcontinental airway, most of it in the big sky over the western mountains. Certainly my view from the ninth floor of 25 Broadway was not quite so spectacular. Although Manhattan possesses a special majesty of its own—being an island of tall masonry surrounded by waterways that abound with big and little shipping—it is seldom arranged that such a glamorous scene is visible to a junior executive. My own special panorama was always the same in fair weather and foul. A few yards away a tall wall of sooty brown brick reared toward the unseen heavens. The dreary brick was broken at intervals by large, curtainless windows, where other nine-to-five prisoners could be seen working the adjacent anthill.

This was a mountain pilot's penance for poking an inquisitive nose into grandiose international matters, such as flying big airliners across the Atlantic. It stemmed from a rumor that pervaded the western mountains early in 1938—an exciting rumor about a new international airline which would bear the name American Export Airlines. This was to be Pan American Airways' first American-flag competition on any ocean.

It wasn't difficult for an eager pilot to invade Wall Street and pound on the door where this bold idea was being hatched. Inscribed on the frosty glass was the name of one of the street's classiest consulting firms: a collection of business analysts assembled under the resonant title Coverdale and Colpitts. William Coverdale and John Slater, the big bosses of this outfit, were also shipping tycoons, the headmen of American Export Lines which plied the Atlantic and Mediterranean with a sizable collection of freighters and passenger liners.

Here in the cement canyons of lower Manhattan a few pioneer aviation men were setting up the new airline. The guiding light of this effort was Jim Eaton, a big name in the air-transport business, who pioneered with Pan American and Ludington Airlines. It was Jim Eaton's idea that a large shipping company with established commercial outlets throughout Europe should fit wings to its boats and thus achieve a swift, new seagoing capability. At this stage of aviation history, landplanes with underslung wheels and leaky bottoms were understandably unpopular when it came to crossing the ocean with passengers. Only flying boats could do the job, and American Export had ordered the construction of three four-engine craft, the most expensive in existence, to fly the Atlantic and Mediterranean.

Jim Eaton was not on hand this particular day, nor was D.G. Richardson who later took charge of operations. It was the youngest of American Export Airlines' pioneer executives who answered my persistent knock. The door cracked a few cagey inches to let a lean-faced, canny-looking fellow pop his head out to cast a piercing eye at the visitor from the western mountains. Then, making sure that no stranger got an unauthorized glance at the Coverdale and Colpitts crystal ball, the head suddenly joined a body which slid mysteriously through the crack to meet me in the dark hallway.

This was Tom Jones, Annapolis class of 1928, a naval aviator recently retired because of a disabled starboard eardrum. Among other things it was Tom Jones's job to size up visiting airmen who might be interested in future employment.

Jones was no glad-hander. He came to the point immediately. "What's on your mind?" he snapped, cocking his good ear in my direction so that it could be filled with my reasons for coming.

"Looking for new places to go," I told him. After that I must have filled his ear pretty full. When operations began in 1940 I held the chief pilot's job in the new company, with seniority number one.

Meanwhile, in the summer of 1939, American Export Airlines' first airplane, a twin-engine Consolidated PBY-4 Catalina flying boat called *Transatlantic*, made three round trips across the Atlantic to France, Ireland, and Portugal on route surveys, thus jostling Pan Am which started regular transatlantic service with Boeing 314 clipper flying boats in the same year.

In 1940 *Transatlantic* was poised on the seaplane ramp at Floyd Bennett Field's Coast Guard hangar on the shores of Jamaica Bay near Brooklyn. The Civil Aeronautics Board had granted American Export Airlines, the steamship line's flying subsidiary, a franchise to fly the mails in this twin-engine craft between New York and Lisbon, Portugal, until the three four-engine flying boats under construction at Sikorsky would be ready for daily flights from New York to the Mediterranean with passengers, mail, and cargo.

My first task in the summer of 1940 was to hire a pair of flight crews, and to train them toward keeping the *Transatlantic* airborne on a projected weekly mail service to Lisbon via Horta in the Azores. This job was disposed of by converting a pair of transcontinental pilots, Dick Mitchell and Dick McMakin of United Air Lines, into salt-water aviators. In the process we splashed around the Atlantic, Caribbean, and Gulf of Mexico circuit, dropping into New Orleans, Havana, and Belize, and Nassau, Kingston, and Cristobal.

At every port of call our public relations experts excited the local chamber of commerce by promising to start new airline services all over the map, although there was only one company airplane, the lumbering *Transatlantic,* visible to the naked eye. Thus our outfit lapped up a great deal of premature publicity as we hauled newshawks around and about under towering cumulus, across jungles and deep blue seas into coral-reefed harbors.

This was good flying, but all the while the big chiefs back home in New York were taking a beating in their effort to steer the airline east toward a quarreling Europe, rather than south where the commercial airline scene was less glamorous to behold.

On the western side of the Atlantic, the infant airline had convinced almost everyone it should be allowed to fly —except for a couple of powerful dissenters. Pan American Airways, America's pioneer overseas airline, was understandably unhappy about interlopers trespassing its transatlantic domain. Being unsophisticated about these matters, we hardly noticed the fingers pressing our tender young Adam's apple. But it wasn't long before we woke up to discover our cherished mail service to Lisbon had been impolitely choked off.

Those indelicate fingers caressing our well-squeezed throat turned out to be Portuguese. Pan Am, for good and valid reasons, just chuckled heartily on the sidelines. The Lisboners saw no need for two competing American airlines splashing in their river Tagus. All the while the State Department, which should have been in charge of such matters, looked the other way with an eye on bigger problems. Adolf Hitler was campaigning through Europe all the way to the Pyrenees.

While the Portuguese massaged our windpipe, the Congress of the United States delivered a sharp blow to the solar plexus. Our government-sponsored franchise to fly the transatlantic mails needed Congressional action to produce the funds that would help pay the cost. By a margin of one vote the Senate Appropriations Committee almost wiped us out.

But the attack on Pearl Harbor changed all this. Anyone who owned a large airplane was loaded with transportation potential—especially an outfit almost ready to launch a fleet of four-engine flying boats with the hitherto unheard of capability of flying nonstop across the Atlantic.

In mid-January of 1942 the first of these flying boats was ready for its maiden test flight. I was scheduled to be the test pilot for this new Sikorsky, and it was the first time I would be testing a new airplane fresh from the drawing boards. The assignment promised to be an absorbing and exciting affair.

My feeling for this big seaplane, technically known as an S-44, had by now become affectionate and possessive. I had watched it grow from a mere keel to a beautiful flying boat, to what we expected would be the fastest of all, with the longest cruising range. Day after day, as I suffered through the growing pains of this winged ship, it gradually became *my* airplane.

On January 17 a special train sped up the New Haven rails from New York to Bridgeport with a trainload of top aviation brass en route to the Sikorsky plant at Stratford, Connecticut, where they would witness the christening of this big transatlantic flying boat. I was on that train, too, perhaps feeling less festive than the rest because my thoughts were riveted on test-flying my big seaplane.

One of the first items on the day's agenda was the smashing of a bottle of champagne across the new ship's bow. Mrs. Henry Wallace, wife of the Vice President of the United States, was on hand for this task. After several lusty swings the bottle was finally fractured, and the airplane officially named *Excalibur*. It was the first of a long line of *Excalibur*s I would be destined to fly.

The Sikorsky was the second vessel flying the American Export flag to bear the name of the legendary sword of King Arthur. The first was an ocean liner which would soon be sent to the bottom of the Atlantic off the coast of North Africa, victim of a German torpedo.

The weather on this January day was cold, but bright and sunny, and I was hoping the christening and speech-making wouldn't use up too much of the afternoon. I wanted to take advantage of the last precious hours of daylight for putting the airplane through its first paces.

But it was not to be. The festivities went on until the sun was too low in the western sky for any test flying.

It was on the following afternoon that the new flying boat faced its moment of truth. I climbed into the left front seat, and Dick Mitchell, as copilot, took over the right side of the cockpit. *Excalibur* was then eased gently down the Sikorsky ramp into the ice-rimmed Housatonic River.

I eyed the clock impatiently during the slow and tedious

process of removing the beaching gear. In January the days aren't long enough, and there was much work to be done.

Big stakes would be riding with me on this first day.

After some preliminary slow-speed maneuvers it was my intention to taxi at high speed on the step. In hydroplaning position I could get a feel for the airplane's hull characteristics and the effectiveness of its controls. But this big boat was livelier than any I had ever flown. It accelerated like a startled greyhound, and at seventy-five knots I suddenly became aware we were no longer bumping gently across the wavelets. We were airborne.

Excalibur was flying, but without my permission!

"Where do you think you're going?" I muttered. "You're not going to fly me, my friend—I'm going to fly you."

I pulled off the power, and made extra sure my willful flying machine landed gracefully from its maiden airborne excursion. There was no difficulty with the length of runway. Long Island Sound is a hundred miles long.

After slowing down in the water, I accelerated onto the step again. This time there would be discipline. I pulled back on the controls. *Excalibur* obeyed. Once again we were airborne.

The uncertainties of all those months of waiting and watching were wiped out. I enjoyed the heady moment to the full. It was impossible to resist sharing it, so I flew low over the Sikorsky factory to show all hands what a beautiful, magnificent airplane they had created.

After four months of intensive tests, mostly from the Naval Air Station at Jacksonville, Florida, this newest of flying boats earned its license and began flying the Atlantic to Ireland on its shakedown flights, setting new standards of speed and range for ocean-going aircraft. Then, on the twenty-second of June, 1942, this latest of flying ships to span the Atlantic made its first westbound crossing out of Foynes, Ireland, with passengers and mail.

This big ship and its two sisters had long since been committed to fly for the Navy between New York and Foynes under the guise of the commercial airline that created them—American Export Airlines. The neutral port of Foynes, a sleepy Irish village on the south bank of the river Shannon, ranked in the war years as one of the world's foremost air terminals. Here the flying boats of Pan American, British Overseas Airways, and American Export Airlines embarked and disembarked the high and low brass of the allied war effort.

We set out from Foynes on this longest of summer days, without any special ambition. The big Sikorsky's fuel tanks were a few hundred gallons short of their 3,820 gallon capacity when the seaplane slipped her mooring to ease into the riptide that raced through the narrow west channel between Foynes Island and the south bank of the Shannon. The flight plan called for a fuel stop at Botwood in Newfoundland, on the Bay of Exploits—some fourteen hours away.

An onlooker on the shore might have thought this heavily laden flying boat was more likely to go to the bottom of the broad river rather than fly safely across the ocean. The hull was so deeply submerged by the full load that the passenger windows were only inches above water level. At the beginning of takeoff a huge wave flared out from the bow to enshroud the ship so heavily with spray that only the wing tips and top of the tail were visible. Finally, seeking release from its briny surroundings, the hull lumbered heavily onto the step at a mile a minute clip and began to skim across the water toward its hundred mile an hour takeoff speed.

On this cool June evening a brisk west wind streaked the waters of Ireland's fabled river Shannon. I pulled back strenuously on the controls as *Excalibur* climbed quickly into hydroplaning position, then swept majestically down river toward Loop Head and the North Atlantic.

R.B.I.T.S.—D

On this voyage my crew was unusually heavy with airline wisdom. Along for some practical training were four senior airline captains whose total flying experience probably exceeded any like grouping ever before assembled on a flight deck. In the copilot's seat was Captain Bob Hixson, one of the best aviators I know and a veteran of United's transcontinental. Hixson had a head start over the others. He had been flying with me during the S-44 tests at Jacksonville and had already been fully purged of any inclination toward landplanes.

Sixteen passengers occupied the Sikorsky's spacious passenger cabin—two to each stateroom. They included Britain's famed combat admiral and commander of the Mediterranean Fleet, Sir Andrew Cunningham. The admiral was on his way to Washington to help arrange the invasion of North Africa. Along, too, were a couple of ambassadors and some other top brass. The host in the passenger cabin was purser Bill Scouler, a miniature Scot who was assisted by stewardess Dorothy Bohanna, R.N. —the first stewardess to fly any ocean.

This first scheduled westbound flight of American Export Airlines promised to be a long voyage, but the passenger accommodations were much more plush than those of the latter-day landplanes. Nor did the crew members suffer. We could take turns easing the fatigue problem in the berths up forward, below the flight deck.

Although there was a war going on, most of our ocean-flying hazards stemmed from the winds and weather. However, later in the war, when flying closer to Europe across the Bay of Biscay to and from Portugal and North Africa, there would be occasional fireworks from a German submarine.

But I was shot at only once during three years of wartime flying. This was to the west of Lisbon, in the early dawn, and the submariners may have been as surprised as we were. But they had the ammunition, and we had none.

The enemy fighter-interceptors never bothered any of the flying boats, although some British landplane airliners were less lucky. Our ocean-hugging flying boats always managed to hide from hostile radar eyes scanning the Bay of Biscay from the coastline of France and Spain.

There was little man-made trouble in the air over the North Atlantic, but we sometimes encountered victims of well-aimed torpedoes burning fiercely on the surface of the windblown ocean, lighting up the night for miles around.

On this particular June night the war seemed to be elsewhere. *Excalibur* rumbled peacefully through the darkness a thousand feet above the sea. The only evidence of the ocean's presence was the faint luminescence of wind-tossed whitecaps which appeared vaguely as tumbling crescents unfolding toward the westerlies that created them.

The big hull, suspended from a wide span of wing, occasionally trembled slightly in the ripple of wind and cloud, but at a hundred and thirty knots on the airspeed indicator there was no discomfort in this gentle motion.

On the flight deck Harry Lamont was in charge of navigation, and his first concern was to guarantee accurate course. Now and then he made his way aft toward the stern where he would toss out a smoke bomb that would burn on the surface of the sea to allow the measurement of drift.

We dead reckoned below the clouds until past mid-ocean, using only the airspeed, compass, and drift flares for guidance. But dead reckoning wasn't enough. More exact information was needed, which called for a glimpse of the heavens. So, though it cost some fuel, we struggled up to eight thousand feet, where a sky-full of stars told us exactly where we were.

Mike Doyle, the chief flight engineer, kept himself

awake matching his fuel records against the navigational score. An effervescent Irishman with a twinkle in the eye and a gray fringe around his bald head, Mike exuded great physical power. He was short and stocky, and sturdy as a fire hydrant. This seagoing craftsman and retired chief aviation machinist mate had learned his trade during a twenty-three-year hitch in the Navy. Along with his airborne duties, he was capable of fixing anything that needed to be fixed on a flying boat—from splicing a line or mending a hole in the bottom to changing an engine at a wind-blown, wave-tossed mooring.

There was little to disturb the stillness of the night watch except the chatter of the radio operator's transmitting bug which sputtered Morse code into the four corners of the ocean. While on duty all radio operators seem like men from another planet, withdrawn into a world of their own which speaks a twittering language of dashes and dots.

On this trip Mike McFarlen was chief radio operator. A slim and dour Texan, Mike's usually solemn face could flash an engaging smile when things were going right.

But his face was more solemn than usual. His deep pile of radio messages describing the threatening weather in Newfoundland gave him nothing to smile about. I noticed his long, thin face become more melancholy.

"Skipper, it's going to be socked in," McFarlen finally announced in a mournful twang.

The surface wind at Botwood, where we were scheduled to land for fuel, had veered to the northeast, blowing in a blanket of drizzle and fog from the ocean, covering Botwood's Bay of Exploits and the alternate landing area at Gander Lake.

The radio operator was merely saying out loud what I had been thinking during the past few hours.

Where could we take on some gasoline?

Beyond Newfoundland the next seaplane base that

boasted a fueling barge was at Shediac in the Canadian Maritimes. Shediac, near Moncton in New Brunswick was a first-class haven for flying boats. But our weather messages indicated this harbor, too, would be heavily fogged in during the hours we could use it.

Halifax, therefore, was the final resort, although there was nothing certain about this harbor on Nova Scotia's east coast. Yet the fog there would surely be thinned into less troublesome smog by the steepening rays of the summer sun. There should be enough visibility for a safe landing.

Because Newfoundland was clearly a lost cause we altered course a few degrees left to pass to seaward of Cape Race at its southeastern tip. For several hours we had been soaring smoothly above softly luminous clouds under a canopy of stars, lapping up the luxury of precise celestial navigation.

But this easygoing flying above the clouds was courting trouble. A reddish pinpoint of light in the western sky was gradually telling us we were encountering some forceful resistance. Aldebaran, the red star hanging directly over *Excalibur*'s nose between a dimly lit Pleiades and the gaudy spread of Orion, was sensing an intolerable headwind that would bite deeply into our fuel reserves.

"These speed lines* show we've made thirty miles in the last thirty minutes," Harry Lamont declared glumly. "That means we've got eighty knots on the nose. Our groundspeed is less than half our airspeed."

Mike Doyle pushed his pencil a few moments. "That's four-tenths of a mile per gallon, and we've got eleven hundred gallons."

"At that rate," I reckoned, "we'll have dry tanks a hundred miles short of Halifax."

* One of the simpler celestial navigation techniques involves the computation of lines of position called speed lines, or course lines. A series of such speed lines taken at intervals can be used for resolving the groundspeed of the aircraft.

"Glad this is a boat," said Hixson.

The only place to improve matters would be down near the surface of the sea. If the ground wind at Botwood was northeasterly, it shouldn't be too much different in the vicinity of Cape Race—which would give us a welcome tailwind.

Because our airplane undoubtedly owned a monopoly of this part of the ocean, McFarlen merely rattled off our intentions in a clatter of dashes and dots. Airway traffic control on the oceans hardly existed those days.

With our new plan declared, we took leave of the hostile upper air and quickly plunged into an envelopment of amorphous mist, which was soon harshened by the rising sun behind us. As we felt our way down through the lowest layer of cloud, the blinding white mists turned to gray, and suddenly we were totally released from the sun-drenched glare to find ourselves beneath the clouds' lowest tendril only a few hundred feet above the blue-black ocean.

It was lucky we hadn't postponed this cloud penetration much longer because the leaden overcast soon sank almost to the tops of the long Atlantic swells. But even though the cloud ceiling was close to the surface of the ocean, we still had to fly high enough to elude the masts of small shipping that might suddenly appear in front of us.

It turned out there was none of the hoped-for northeasterly tailwind near the surface, but at least we were free of the ill-mannered headwinds that cost so much fuel. The Sikorsky rode smoothly along on a windless cushion of ocean air, and at this low altitude it was a bonanza worth a few drums of gasoline. The cushion of air between the flying boat's big wings and the surface of the sea allowed such a substantial reduction of fuel flow to our thirsty engines that the fuel records would surely agitate the slide rules of our engineering friends back home. We reduced the r.p.m.'s as low as we could and still stay efficiently airborne. The noise of propellers and engine became a whisper.

Excalibur skimmed over the swells, clocking one hundred and ten knots. The visibility ahead was scant, but it was enough. We felt secure in our knowledge that the big icebergs were astern, and that the tall cliffs of Cape Race would pass a comfortable distance to starboard. Nor was there much to worry about from big shipping. The big ocean vessels seldom cruised in this domain of the bluenose fisherman.

Flying close to the rolling swells demanded alert attention, and kept everyone on the flight deck wide-awake. The hours ground away into monotonous infinity until we became hardly conscious of the sound of the engines. Finally, the windless sea was broken by a patch of rock-studded whitecaps.

"Land ho!" Hixson announced, much as Columbus must have said it on the poop deck of the *Santa Maria*.

For the huge continent of North America, it was certainly a niggardly landfall, but for us it was *land*. The northeastern cape of fog-smitten Nova Scotia was less than a mile away, yet it was totally invisible.

Although sandwiched tightly between cloud and ocean, we had enough visibility to dodge any obstruction that might loom ahead. Nor did the mists of the morning dampen a new prospect. At our first landfall we had as many gallons of fuel remaining as there were miles to go to New York. I was beginning to toy with the idea of flying nonstop.

The Pratt and Whitney engines churned smoothly at thirteen hundred revolutions per minute, burning a gallon of fuel for each nautical mile that slipped under the keel, and I knew that this fuel versus mileage factor would improve slightly as the airplane further unburdened its fuel tonnage.

We held course close to shore, but the only visible evidence of the low-lying coastline was an occasional sea-swept rock that jutted from the coastal shallows.

From Nova Scotia's northeastern promontory, it would be an hour and a half to Halifax, the last place before New York where we could get fuel out of a hose. The cloud ceiling at Halifax was reported to be close to the surface of the sea, but this posed no difficult problem. We were already under the overcast. All we needed was a radio bearing when offshore the entrance to the harbor. Then we could turn and fly along it among the shipping to the landing area.

But there was a problem about Halifax that landplane pilots would scarcely appreciate. The bottom of the flying boat, being of thin metal, was vulnerable to floating debris. Three days ago, while eastbound, we paused at Halifax for extra fuel before undertaking the long flight to Ireland. The harbor was infested with a scattering of small pieces of lumber which were barely visible above the greasy, glassy surface. During the landing and takeoff among a clutter of shipping it was necessary to swerve the big seaplane to right and left to escape the menacing debris.

This was a repelling consideration, and it conspired with our newly discovered fuel thrift. I was slowly abandoning the idea of landing *anywhere* short of New York.

We had been aloft twenty hours since the last glimpse of land at Loop Head near the mouth of the Shannon. Twenty hours of fuel records had to be thoroughly double-checked before I could commit the Sikorsky to the five-hour extension to New York.

"Mike," I said, "let's recheck all those flow meter records since Foynes—double-check 'em. Maybe we'll go all the way."

The engineer gave a questioning look, and then his eyes lit up. "Yes, sir! I'll have it in a couple of minutes."

Hixson added his approval. "Now you're talking, Charlie."

"Mac, get a reading on the Boston and New York weather."

McFarlen flashed a smile for the first time in twenty hours.

The flight deck came alive.

It turned out that the fuel records agreed with the less dependable fuel gauges, and we were clearly gaining a little on the fuel-versus-miles score. We now possessed a few more gallons of fuel than there were miles to go.

Our ace in the hole was a sight gauge full of gasoline. It was a vertical glass tube fastened to a hundred-gallon reserve tank above the aft end of the flight deck. This was the last tank we would be using, and it was reassuring to actually see the gasoline. When the fuel started descending in that glass tube we could fly one hundred miles more, and that would be all.

I let Halifax slip invisibly by as if it wasn't there, but this didn't mean I was going for broke on this last lap to New York. There were various small harbors and a couple of big ones up ahead that could offer safe anchorage. I could even land safely in the open ocean without suffering any damage except to the ego.

The idea of terminating this voyage anywhere between Halifax and New York was painful to contemplate. Our competitors would be greatly amused to see us put on an amateur performance. Even worse, although the high brass in the passenger cabin had been admirably cheerful thus far, the mood would certainly chill if we dropped down in some remote cove.

But, if the westerly surface wind didn't freshen too much, the big S-44 would be setting a new transatlantic standard before she was fastened to her mooring at New York's marine terminal at La Guardia Airport.

New York's Whitestone Bridge was silhouetted beneath the afternoon sun when we switched to the tank that showed the final hundred gallons of fuel. Our press agents had been boasting for years about flying nonstop across the Atlantic. Now this was about to happen—the first time for an airliner with passengers and mail.

We climbed above the big span just to make sure everyone was aware this was an airplane, not a surface vessel—if anyone was beginning to wonder.

The fuel tank showed ninety-five gallons when Mike Doyle looped the mooring hawser around the bow post. This was enough, though it was only a tiny fraction of the gasoline we lifted off the river Shannon twenty-five hours and forty minutes before landing on Flushing Bay.

"Remarkable voyage" was the British Navy's crisp analysis when Admiral Cunningham disembarked, and the glint in his eye suggested he wasn't being loose with his praise.

But it would have been just another ocean flight with a fuel stop if that red star in the sky—Aldebaran—hadn't flagged us down out of the headwinds.

CHAPTER THREE

A Myth Vanishes

Aviation myths die hard, but the requirements of war often help speed them on their way. *Excalibur*'s nonstop Atlantic journey was only the beginning.

Starting a full-scale international airline from scratch, without any nucleus of personnel, and with a big war going on, presented some difficult aspects. Where, for instance, would the pilots come from, bearing in mind that only the best and most experienced could do the job?

American Export Airlines' contract with the Navy called for fulfilling a large share of the Navy's air transport needs on the North Atlantic. Such a job would be no soft touch for any airline. For a brand-new outfit about to be deluged with fifteen large flying boats, it promised to be touch and go.

Our toughest task would be the taming of the North Atlantic winter. Before 1942 the winter weather on this boisterous ocean had been pronounced too severe for the operation of airliners, especially flying boats. But now, with the new Sikorsky, we had a ship that could fly more non-stop miles than any airliner before it. With this extra cruising range we could go out and try to dispel some myths about the North Atlantic.

But it would take a team of the most proficient airline pilots to do the job, men who could navigate as well as fly. These pilots, besides being ocean navigators, would need to be expert at all kinds of bad-weather flying, either by quick reference to landmarks when skimming beneath the overcast in bad visibility, or by the more modern technique of resorting to instruments and radio while penetrating low clouds to a landing.

Moreover, once landed, the big winged ships needed good seamen at the helm. They required skillful handling in tricky winds, waves, and tides. A landlubber, accustomed to the easy-going simplicity of wheel brakes on dry land, could easily wreck a flying boat just fumbling around on the surface.

Finally, the number-one characteristic a chief pilot looks for in his men is *air sense*. Though resourceful and aggressive, the best pilots also know when to take the pressure off.

All these qualities added up to a pilot who scarcely existed.

Pan American Airways had a group of them, master ocean pilots like Harold Gray who commanded the *Yankee Clipper* on its pioneer transatlantic journey in 1939. Another of this select group was Captain Marius "Lodi" Lodeesen, who many years later would help me set up an interisland seaplane service in the Caribbean.

But Pan Am was off-limits. I would need to look elsewhere for my own crop of ocean pilots.

There were others who shared my misgivings about the

availability of qualified aviators. Back in December of 1941, a month before the launching of the first big Sikorsky, Admiral John Towers, one of the Navy's original airmen who became chief of the Bureau of Aeronautics, summoned me to Washington to tell him who would be at the controls of his new flying ships.

It took some fast talk to placate him. Luckily he was never really aware of the fact that my bag of qualified aviators was so empty. The three pilots we counted on most to help get things started—the men I trained on the twin-engine *Transatlantic* in the Caribbean—were gone from the scene. McMakin was killed in a B-24 at San Diego. Tom Terrill was a prisoner of the Japanese, captured in the Philippines. Mitchell had landed a big job with another company.

But the transcontinental airlines had plenty of good pilots who possessed the more urgent qualifications we were looking for. These men had long since acquired all they needed in the way of air sense, and they knew how to fly the weather. Seamanship and ocean navigation could be taught fairly quickly to able and experienced men.

But this kind of pilot was glued to the left seat of his DC-3 cockpit by seniority, and by the best of pay and working conditions. It would take a good lure to catch him.

Excalibur, of course, was good bait. There was a dramatic combination of grace and power in the lines of her wings and hull. She was a ship with plenty of class.

But some live bait was needed, too—a Pied Piper of sorts—to help me separate many of the best airline pilots in the United States from their high pay and job security, to persuade them to start all over again in a new and unsure environment. I needed a prominent airline pilot whose credentials included long experience and the best of rapport with his fellow pilots in the airline industry.

Along at the right moment came a friend and flying

colleague from United Air Lines: Cameron T. Robertson. Robby could hardly wait to fling off the sedate security of his check pilot status in San Francisco to seek new horizons on the Atlantic.

With *Excalibur* on exhibit, and Robertson to help me rope in the pilots, the shortage of qualified men quickly became an overabundance. Dozens of the best transcontinental airline pilots put in their bid to fly the Atlantic. Nor could anything frighten them off, not even the tales of utter gloom I spun about the future of this fledgling airline.

Close behind Robertson came three of United Air Lines's high-ranking chief pilots; Emery Martin, Charlie Thompson, and Bob Bergesen, the flight managers at New York, Chicago, and Los Angeles. Bergesen was one of the mountain pilots I had flown with almost a decade before. Along, too, came a dozen others among United's best men, together with several from Eastern. I nursed hopes that my ex-boss and friend W. A. "Pat" Patterson, United's able chief executive, would forgive this act of piracy. These were the kind of men who could take an airplane over the horizon and I could be sure they'd come back.

There was a good crop of copilots, too, headed by Bob Neale, top-ranking ace of the Flying Tigers with sixteen victories over the Japanese.

This left me with little to worry about in the flying department. Therefore I had time left over to take my own turn in the North Atlantic schedule, and concentrate on the winter weather problems.

At the beginning we found it prudent to probe discreetly at the North Atlantic winter from the southern side of the Gulf Stream. This involved heading southeast for an intermediate fuel stop at Bermuda before pointing the nose toward Ireland.

But before long, enough was learned about the mid-ocean winter to consider flying the Atlantic eastbound the year round in one flight—thirty-one hundred miles nonstop from New York to Ireland. I made this proposal to the top management, and the new routing was accepted.

We flew the more southerly rhumb-line track at first, to allow an easier escape into the Azores or Lisbon if the wintry air mass on the north side of the Gulf Stream became too formidable. But eventually, after gathering a year of experience, the Sikorskys were simply flown throughout the winter on the track that yielded the best winds, wherever the best wind component happened to be, which was sometimes far to the north of the great circle.

The myth about North Atlantic invincibility in winter thus became a casualty of the war. It would eventually be laid completely to rest by long-range landplanes.

There had been urgent reasons for resolving our route problem besides the need to expedite our naval air-transport function. The majority of seaplanes flying the Atlantic —the Boeing 314s of Pan American and British Overseas Airways—possessed less range than our Sikorskys, but they were authorized by the Portuguese to fly the less direct route to Ireland via the Azores and Lisbon in better weather. At the same time our flying boats were denied entry into these Portuguese domains except in an emergency, or when forced to land by adverse winds or weather.

But this Portuguese snag turned out to be a boon instead. The ocean swells outside the tiny harbor at Horta in the Azores could batter a flying boat to submission while attempting to take off with a heavy load of fuel. The long wait at Horta for the swells to subside often made a shambles of winter transatlantic schedules.

But even the long-legged Sikorskys couldn't safely tackle the big winter westerlies on the direct route *westbound* from Ireland to New York. There was no harbor in the Canadian Maritimes that could reliably offer an ice-free takeoff or landing. Nor was it prudent to cruise at low altitude against the vigorous winter headwinds. The clouds near the surface of the sea were too often saturated with subcooled moisture that froze and clung to every protuberance on the airplane. Icing was a dread problem those days.

Therefore, the homeward voyage to New York from Ireland after mid-October called for a detour that touched down on four continents. This winter journey via the South Atlantic covered almost triple the distance of the direct flight from New York to Foynes. The first leg was southward —three thousand miles nonstop across the Bay of Biscay to Portugal, thence along the coast of French Morocco, Spain's Rio del Oro, and France's Senegal to British Gambia.

In 1942 there wasn't much en route hospitality on this southward leg of the journey. The Bay of Biscay was a domain of the *Luftwaffe* and German U-boats. The French territories were responsive to a hostile Pétain in Vichy. The Spaniards, too, would give us less than pleasant greeting if forced to land. Altogether too much of Africa was under control of the enemy, which caused us to fly beyond Dakar to find a benevolent coastline. This ribbon of beach marked the approach to Bathurst in British Gambia.

At Bathurst the Sikorsky dropped down on the Gambia River at a West African roost of Britain's Royal Air Force. This obscure West African port near the Equator was much farther away from New York than our point of origin on the river Shannon. But the temperature, both political and atmospheric—our reason for coming—was friendly.

At Bathurst the route to New York took a right-angle turn, heading west across the South Atlantic. It was twenty hours to Port of Spain in Trinidad, or a little less air time to Belém on the Amazon when the passenger load proved too heavy for the longer trip. Occasionally, when load permitted, the Sikorsky stretched its legs all the way from West Africa to Puerto Rico on the north fringe of the Caribbean, some twenty-three hours away.

This was airline flying at its best, and it was always a

letdown to return to New York and find headaches in the New York office that no bottle of aspirin could fix. As we acquired more airplanes from the Navy, a batch of younger, less proven pilots had to be appointed to command them.

It wasn't easy to peer into a stranger's psyche and try to measure his common-sense factor. Because the new men were relatively unknown, with little or no background of command, it took some guesswork to sort them out. The result wasn't altogether perfect.

Checking out pilots in landplanes is never so much of a problem. But flying boats are different. For every takeoff and landing, the pilot must build his own airport out of a new combination of winds and waves. Even the chore of tying up to a mooring can be a frustrating task.

Although our company's safety record was good for seaplanes, we still lost two of them. Both times the captains were the youngest and least experienced, trying to match the performance of the old pros, but with a lesser store of knowledge to keep them out of trouble.

A big Coronado PB2Y was smashed in two at Dakar by a heavy swell, unseen during a takeoff on a black night. All but one of the passengers survived.

But it was the other accident that broke the hearts of everyone around. It destroyed *Excalibur,* the flagship of our fleet, and half the passengers and crew, including our great Irishman, Mike Doyle, went down with her.

Shortly before sundown of an evening in early October the big Sikorsky was gunned from the dock at Botwood, Newfoundland, to fly the short distance to Gander Lake to pick up more passengers and a load of fuel. It was Indian summer in Newfoundland, and the Bay of Exploits showed hardly a ripple. The lightly fueled ship climbed quickly onto the step for its takeoff run.

But something was clearly wrong. The hull buried its nose ever deeper as it gathered speed, and for good reason. Somehow—no one will ever know exactly why—the electrically actuated wing flaps had been driven all the way down, and were fully extended.

With the wing flaps so positioned, and with four engines blasting at takeoff power, the nose-heavy forces on the big airplane's elevator could not be controlled by mortal man.

Excalibur's salvation demanded that the pilot throttle back the engines. The lives of passengers and crew depended on such action.

The nose buried deeper and deeper. But the pilot decided he could muscle his winged boat from the possessive sea. He was a big man and his muscles bulged as he pulled mightily back on the elevator control. The throttles went untouched.

The dynamic force of water on the burrowing hull suddenly took over, thrusting the bow of the big ship upward like a harpooned whale. It hovered in midair for an agonizing moment below stalling speed, then plunged steeply into the sea with a thundering crash. The four flailing propellers sent up geysers of spray as the roar of the engines was silenced.

When the great tumult of water subsided, the last rays of the setting sun sparkled on the wavelets of an empty sea. *Excalibur* lay on the bottom of the Bay of Exploits.

CHAPTER FOUR

In Search of Gold

The fastest flying-boat crossing of the Atlantic took place in October 1944, and was clocked in fourteen hours and seventeen minutes for the thirty-one hundred mile flight from New York to Foynes.

This swift journey was flown nonstop in a sister ship of *Excalibur,* and I was the pilot and lucky beneficiary of the tailwinds which chopped an hour and thirteen minutes off the existing transatlantic record. The strong westerlies that propelled this autumnal crossing were found in the southern remnants of a lusty hurricane which had migrated to the North Atlantic by way of the east coast of the United States, where it left a path of wreckage all the way from the Carolinas to Nantucket.

Setting a transatlantic speed record with a large margin to spare is stimulating to an aviator's ego, and gives him a possessive feeling about *his* ocean. I was no exception to this rule.

But it wasn't long before the transatlantic landplanes came along to shatter my sense of possession into small fragments. I viewed this high-handed intrusion of my domain by rubber-tired, dust-blowing vehicles with a jealous eye, and I resolved to do something about it some day.

But it would take a few years. Meanwhile I would need to coin some money.

After World War II my regular job of flying airliners back and forth across the Atlantic to Europe was still going on, minus the military trappings and the chief pilot's desk. But the airline job, now changed from seaplanes to landplanes, was just making me a living. I would need to look elsewhere for "off-airways" money.

In the autumn of 1945 the roots of the new "nonscheduled" airline industry were beginning to take hold. A horde of airplane pilots were taking leave of the armed forces, and thousands of military aircraft of every description were being bulldozed into junk, or released more or less intact to the government war-surplus organization for sale or lease.

During my spare time from scheduled airline flying with American Overseas Airlines I became involved with a small, nonscheduled company which was on the verge of leasing one of these war-weary airplanes. This diversion into new territory was at the invitation of Ralph Cox, a part-time dentist and copilot I had employed back in 1942 when hiring crews to man the flying boats of American Export Airlines.

The first meeting, attended by a gathering of Wall Street and aviation people, was held in New York at the Yale Club.

The main theme of the new company was to introduce

Topper, the Flying Lobster to the gourmets of New York, Chicago, Los Angeles, and every other significant city the length and breadth of the United States. The lobsters would originate in the waters lapping the state of Maine where the more elite American lobsters are alleged to hail from. Our first intention was to flood the restaurants of New York with this crustacean produce. After that the sky would be the limit. Being innocent about such transactions I was certain the only conceivable snag in the plan was the possibility these cold water creatures could not spawn, and grow rapidly enough to fill the cavernous insides of our sky-full of airplanes.

However, to get things started each of the pioneer members was expected to make enough of an initial investment to rent and furnish a suitable office in the financial district. This fiscal sacrifice seemed reasonable enough in view of the gold mine just over the horizon. Maine lobsters, we were sure, would soon become as common as hamburger.

My background as an airline administrator with American Export Airlines qualified me as vice-president, even though I was vice-president of nothing in particular and only one of many executives in a company that could boast only one airplane. However, being a vice-president for the first time gives one a feeling of having arrived.

Additional grandeur came with the new office at 9 Maiden Lane, certainly an appropriate address for any new enterprise. The handsome rug, I liked to think, was part of my contribution. This office was a place where our large executive staff could gather to scheme, and when interest lagged, await fresh inoculations of zeal from the fellow who originally hatched the idea.

After months of talkative meetings our most important achievement was to come up with a copyrighted trade mark portraying a lobster doffing his top hat and smiling, as only Topper, the Flying Lobster could smile.

But too much talk, and too little action, soon convinced

me that Topper, the Flying Lobster would never displace the hamburger industry. He would live to a ripe old age in his cold-water crevices along the coast of Maine.

So I shed my exalted title, and reduced the clutter of executives—lamenting only that handsome rug left behind at 9 Maiden Lane.

I wasn't the only one to make this discouraging discovery. My friend, Dr. Cox, who had invited me into this top-heavy scheme, became convinced even sooner than I that there was little gold to be panned in the Maiden Lane diggings. Therefore, he went forth and leased his own twin-engine C-47, which was quickly converted into a commercial DC-3 that bulged with seating capacity. With this airplane he made a small fortune between New York and Miami where hordes of sun-seeking passengers clambered with wild abandon aboard anything that could stagger off the ground during that bleak winter.

After finding a winter bonanza with his DC-3 on the New York to Miami circuit, the venturesome dentist decided to graduate from DC-3s into bigger, four-engine airplanes. With this in mind the doctor and I, together with a trusty flight engineer, journeyed into Connecticut one spring day in search of an abandoned airfield known as Windsor Locks. This airport was later destined to become the official airport for Hartford.

But in 1946 this particular airport was not much to look at. A casual passer-by would have had difficulty finding the place at all, so massive were the undergrowth and weeds that concealed it from the highway.

Once having found the airfield there was nothing to bar trespass. No watchman guarded the entrance, nor was any living creature in evidence except the occasional jack rabbit bounding here and there along the decomposing runways. Weeds sprouted abundantly between cracks in the pavement.

But to the more professional observer there were two

other landmarks which identified this ghostlike airport for what it used to be.

Close at hand near the airfield entrance, a dilapidated control tower reared skyward a modest few yards, its last vestige of paint gone with the wind and the weather. But I looked in vain for an occupant of the tinted-glass box atop the weather-beaten underpinnings. It would have been in keeping with the deserted scene if a ghost suddenly rose up behind the glass to warn us against any further penetration of the premises.

But the other landmark brought us back to reality. It was an airplane—a four-engine transport known in military lingo as a C-54, series B.

Here was the object of our quest. This would be Cox's forthcoming entry into big-time air transportation.

It stood forlornly at the far end of the airport, the once-shiny skin tarnished and dull, its Air Corps markings stripped away. Branded as war surplus at the tender age of two years, and stripped of its proud insignia, the shabby relic appeared dispossessed and forsaken.

From a distance and in these seedy surroundings its airworthiness looked altogether dubious. However, on closer inspection, the vital components appeared somewhat more trustworthy. This was encouraging to me because my reason for being there was to fly it away.

The flight engineer clambered from wing to wing and from bow to stern to peer into all the places where trouble could secretly generate. When he had finished, Cox and I invaded the cockpit to strap ourselves onto a pair of tattered seat cushions.

After a couple of thousand hours in the left front seat of a DC-4 I had become well acquainted with all the gadgets and with the technique for squeezing this sizable airplane on to a four-thousand-foot runway, such as Roosevelt Field on Long Island where we intended to go.

The flight engineer verified everything was well bolted

together, and the wheels mounted in reliable rubber. The tanks also contained a modest fuel supply, and there was oil in each engine. Much to our surprise the four engines started promptly and ran at an even tempo.

We took leave, and gave Windsor Locks back to the jack rabbits.

There was no hangar at Roosevelt Field that could contain the monster, but the idea of such splendid comfort, and expense, would have been revolting to Cox, anyway. The conversion of this airplane from "military to civil" would be a fresh-air job.

The going rate at a plush aircraft-modification center for converting a C-54 B to a CAA-licensed DC-4 was upward of a hundred thousand dollars. A homegrown conversion out in the open air, doing without the huge overhead of a factory job, would cost only a fraction of that.

There wasn't much overhead out on Roosevelt Field's concrete ramp. There was no office rent or any doe-eyed stenographer to distract the hired help. When the weather was good the mechanics worked on the airplane's externals. When it rained, there was plenty to be done inside its protective skin. Although the usual clutter of kibitzers and sidewalk superintendents further confused the scene, they usually dispersed when the weather was wet.

Here on this expanse of concrete the military C-54 gradually became a commercial DC-4, but only after a great hustle and bustle during the summer of 1946. For months the airplane was strewn all over the ramp, and it sometimes looked doubtful if the thousands of pieces could ever be put together again. My function would be to test-fly it if that day ever came.

Somehow by summer's end it was ready to go, and I took it aloft on its first test flight. After becoming thoroughly convinced that the airplane was airworthy we dropped in on Long Island's Aviation Country Club at Hicksville for lunch and to demonstrate that an aircraft with four engines doesn't always need a big airport. Besides the tennis courts, swimming pool, and other trimmings, this aviation club sported a grass-covered airfield that was not much more than two thousand feet long.

The landing from north to south in dead calm air was routine, except that the sunbathers didn't think so as they dived hastily into the swimming pool. But taking off from this sod field was more exacting, and we picked up some extra yardage by making a semicircular departure. The takeoff roll was started in a west-southwesterly direction, and we were airborne on a northwesterly heading without trespassing our wheels on the adjacent meadow.

This airplane was clearly capable of great things. The Civil Aeronautics Administration concurred and decorated it with a license and a new number—NC58021. No one took the trouble to shatter a bottle of champagne across its humble prow. It wasn't customary to anoint a mere tramp of the airways.

It was early November, six months after I picked up the airplane at Windsor Locks, before everything was ready. The next order of business was to start making money. Cox's new company, called Ocean Air Tradeways, would need to start flying promptly with its first four-engine payload. On the ground an airplane becomes a leech which can quickly bleed its owner to an agonizing fiscal demise.

The first trip was a big one. NC58021 was contracted to fly all the way to the Persian Gulf, to a land that flowed black gold—Saudi Arabia.

The contract stated that the passengers must be on their way within twenty-four hours. Although this didn't allow much time for assembling a competent flight crew, the required half dozen were gathered on the flight deck at the appointed hour. Each man had driven his own hard bargain with Cox.

Dressed as we were in motley mufti we didn't cut much

of a figure, but this was no collection of baboons. Four of us had managed a few days' leave from American Overseas Airlines. Two of the crew weren't thus entangled with the airlines, but they, too, were professionals.

As occupant of the captain's seat I was the overall boss of this quickly assembled expedition. My main function, other than flying, was to coordinate all aspects of a five-day journey that would average fifteen flying hours a day. The most important requirement, other than safety, was to bring the airplane home as quickly as possible.

The aircraft had been chartered to the Arabian-American Oil Company (Aramco) because Trans World Airlines, the regular means of transit to Arabia, was grounded by a pilots' strike. We had a total of forty passengers, mostly Aramco employees en route to the Arabian oil fields. Along, too, were three Egyptian potentates, who would be our distinguished guests as far as Cairo. The top man in this trio was Nochrachi Pasha, who would be the next premier of Egypt.

Our purser in the passenger cabin was Bill Scouler, a comrade of the flying boats. He was taking a few days off from his catering business to be our one and only cabin attendant. Besides tending his duties as purser, he would double up as steward, nursemaid, and diplomat.

His skill as a diplomat was fortunate. The Pasha was not an understanding passenger. Being unhappy with the austere accommodations he took to storming up and down the cabin aisle most of the night, his head wrapped in a towel to ward off the persistent drafts that attacked him from every nook and corner of NC58021. His two companions could do nothing to calm him down.

We refueled at Stephensville, Newfoundland, and by the time of our arrival over Paris the cabin behind us was in a state of festering turmoil. To make matters worse we were obliged to divert to London after circling for an hour over

Paris, waiting in vain for our turn to land in the ever-thickening fog at Orly.

A diversion to London was usually a routine maneuver, but unfortunately it was past midnight when we arrived. The Pasha had missed a Paris airport rendezvous with some political pals, and this brought forth a new spasm of abuse and agitation.

The landing in London caused other difficulties. Our maps and radio-facility charts for the journey to Arabia were waiting for us in Paris, together with instructions for the routing beyond Cairo. To meet the deadline, we had been obliged to leave New York in a hurry, and no one from Aramco who came to La Guardia Airport knew our final destination—not even the passengers. Just fly toward Arabia, we were told. Someone in Paris would furnish the details.

The phone call from London to Paris availed nothing, so it was decided to start out in the direction of Cairo without delay. Our first order of business was to rid ourselves of the troublesome Pasha. But there was another perplexing problem. Cairo had two airports to choose from—Payne Field and El Almaza. The toss of a coin chose El Almaza.

There were no maps to be had at London Airport in the middle of the night, except for a chart of the route on the controller's wall. However, it was securely pasted there, so the best we could do was to commit it to memory.

We were soon on the road to Cairo, flying a route that kept the western slopes of the Alps at a healthy distance in the darkness. Over Sicily a dazzling sun came up to scorch the windshield as we pushed against strong easterly head-winds toward the Egyptian end of the Mediterranean.

After takeoff at London I had discovered a chart in my flight bag. It was a map of Europe and the Mediterranean which measured some four inches long when plucked from the pages of a small pocket-size memo book. Cunningham, the navigator, had a sharp pencil. While over the sea he plotted celestial-position lines on this miniature map which would have done credit to the navigator of an ocean liner.

The easterly headwind kept me casting an eye on the fuel gauges, but after passing Tobruk I stopped looking. Two hundred gallons would still be in the tanks at Cairo, where the weather promised to be cloudless. It would be difficult to miss the Egyptian capital with so many antiquities jutting out of the landscape, and with the river Nile nearby.

After landing at El Almaza we taxied briskly to a weather-beaten terminal building to park among a clutter of aircraft of all shapes and sizes. But we dared not cut the inboard engines because of a peculiar characteristic of this particular DC-4 while on the ground. Until we could coax some of the passengers to leave their seats and come forward to the cockpit to add weight in the nose, or else find someone outside to install a tall tailpost under the ship's tail, the airplane was so tail-heavy when fully loaded that it would fall back on its tail like a supplicating hound dog as soon as the engines were shut down. This unseemly posture —nose wheel high in the air and tail on the ground—hardly befitted the stars and stripes which decorated the tail of NC58021.

Despite the imposing size of the DC-4, there was little interest in our arrival. An occasional Egyptian gave us a curious stare, but there was no offer of a passenger stairway with which we could dispose of our agonized potentates. After much waving and beckoning, we finally succeeded in making a colorfully uniformed policeman take sufficient notice to signal a cluster of unshaven, skinny-looking workmen, clad in grubby brown coveralls. A small stairway was brought forth which reached halfway to the passenger cabin door. The first step was a long one, but no tears would have been shed in NC58021 if the Pasha had landed upside down on the concrete.

The tailpost was installed and the engines shut down, but it was now clear we had no business at El Almaza. Our high-ranking passenger was certainly not traveling incognito, yet there was no one at this airport to greet him. Obviously his retinue was waiting at Payne Field, a few miles away.

To appease the Pasha I thought about cranking up all the engines and changing airports, but suddenly there was a great shouting and tumult. A thundering stampede of the faithful came storming in from the airport entrance to engulf a black sedan which had somehow materialized at the bottom of the small stairway.

In a few moments the black sedan was gone, and so was the Pasha. He had survived that first step.

After that everything was easy. Someone told us to proceed to a place called Dhahran at the far end of Arabia.

We took leave of Cairo not long after midnight and found ourselves at peace with the world over a vast wasteland that stretched a thousand miles from Suez to the Persian Gulf. Now and then in the star-studded void we spotted a lonely campfire, but there was no other sign of life on the black emptiness of the desert until the dawn came at Dhahran.

The passenger cabin was tranquil. The big shot was gone, and many years later we learned that our agonized traveling companion had, in due course, gone to his reward. He had been assassinated, which was no surprise to anyone. Oddly, none of the crew of NC58021 has ever been accused.

CHAPTER FIVE

Finding a Nugget

One way to catch a tiger by the tail is to start a small airline of your own. It happened to me one June day in 1947 while talking too freely with my friend Jim Eaton. This would be a sideline to my regular flying job with American Overseas Airlines.

The new airline wasn't as substantial as some, being unencumbered with an airplane of any description. Nor did I possess any capital worth mentioning. The Arabian "take" was long gone. Still, these inadequacies were no barrier to getting started. My credit was good, and Jim Eaton's assurance was better than any contract.

Eaton had become vice-president in charge of facilities for American Overseas Airlines, the new name for what had once been American Export Airlines. The Civil Aeronautics Board had decreed that a steamship line could no longer own an airline. Therefore American Airlines, a big domestic company, adopted American Export as a stepchild, and emblazoned their eagle on our fleet of DC-4s and Constellations.

We at American Export had previously forsaken our flying boats for landplanes because airplanes on wheels became popular on the seven seas after Uncle Sam covered the world with concrete and asphalt during World War II. Meanwhile I had parted company with the frustrations that always attend the flying of a boss pilot's desk, and was enjoying the luxury of flying the line. The best relic of my early-bird, chief-pilot realm was possession of seniority number one which unofficially entitled its owner to wear a white uniform shirt instead of the standard blue model.

One of Jim Eaton's areas of responsibility was the company's northern outpost at Keflavik, Iceland. At Keflavik, American Overseas had a link with a big construction outfit known as the Metcalfe, Hamilton, and Kansas City Bridge Company. This company was building hangars and a terminal building at Keflavik's big air base for the Army engineers. Jim Eaton's job, among other things, was to see to it that the construction personnel, tools, and equipment got there safely and quickly.

"We need airlift for three hundred men and their tools from Minneapolis to Iceland," Jim told me. "We're operating every one of our airplanes at peak capacity. Have you got any ideas?"

This was no time to be caught short of a brainstorm. After making a couple of unnecessarily splendid statements I discovered I had started my own airline, unincorporated, unnamed, and unstaffed. It was either that, or welch on those slips of the tongue.

"You can start right away," said Jim, as if my reaction had been expected. "You've got a couple of months. The Bridge Company wants all those men in Iceland by early September."

When in difficulty, a man's first move is usually to find a lawyer. Therefore, to keep everyone on the defensive, I picked one with muscles as well as brains. This big barrister was Francis "Whitey" Wistert, formerly an all-American tackle at the University of Michigan, and a big-league pitcher for Cincinnati who more recently has made football's Hall of Fame.

Within a few days the contract with the Bridge Company was shaped up, and a new airline—Associated Air Transport, Inc.—had thrust a tremulous toe into the non-scheduled airline door. I used the word "associated" because I hoped to prosper as a satellite of American Overseas Airlines where I would continue to fly to make a living.

Because there was no overhead at this stage of the new company's young life, I was able to offer cheap transatlantic rates to my Iceland client. Moreover, with Jim Eaton giving us his vigorous endorsement, the Bridge Company got the extravagant impression we could do no wrong.

One clause in the contract cost me some sleep. I had guaranteed prompt delivery, but was hard-pressed to find an airplane. The big, ocean-going flying machines were in scarce supply.

But the new airline had cash in the bank—one thousand dollars I borrowed to cover odds and ends during the first of ten contract flights to Iceland. This was the acorn I hoped to cultivate into something bigger. Meanwhile all the expensive items, such as airplane rental, fuel bills, maintenance costs and flight pay, would be taken care of after we had been paid for our first flight.

The likeliest aircraft around was Doctor Cox's NC58021, the DC-4 of the previous chapter. But this airplane was so busy it scarcely touched the ground. I could only hope to catch it on the fly.

By snatching it in this manner the first two trips to

Iceland were flown without spectacular problems. But the third scheduled junket found me high and dry without an airplane. NC58021 was in South America when forty of my globe-trotting plumbers, carpenters, and metal workers swarmed off a Minneapolis-to-New York express train, looking for a ride to the Arctic Circle.

If I failed to fulfill the contract schedule I would be responsible for feeding and housing this throng of hungry travelers—an unhappy possibility that could quickly exhaust my company's microscopic treasury. Worse yet, such a fiasco would jolt the ego of this fledgling airline.

To get off this uncomfortable hook, I had been negotiating with an old acquaintance who was in town with a huge Boeing-314 flying boat, one of Pan American Airways' retired Clippers, now owned by another nonscheduled airline. It bore the name *Bermuda Sky Queen* and would become famous before the end of the year by making an unscheduled landing in the middle of the North Atlantic, loaded to capacity with startled passengers who had thought they would be landing in Newfoundland.

My helpful pilot friend, who was temporarily the captain of this big flying boat, was eager to fly our third and most important trip. This was scheduled to be the first trip with payloads in both directions, and therefore it was the first that could put some real meat on our corporate bones. After the regular eastbound contingent was deposited in Iceland, there would be forty Finnish seamen waiting in Stockholm for a ride to New York.

If this round trip could be flown without a big hitch, my new company could breathe a lot easier—a habit not so easy to acquire in this line of work.

The rental price originally quoted for the *Sky Queen* seemed fair enough, and I had been solemnly promised it would be ready to depart from the waters adjacent to Floyd Bennett Airport at the appointed hour. Therefore at nine o'clock in the morning my busload of expectant passengers went trundling to the outskirts of Brooklyn to embark on the big flying ship.

The *Sky Queen* was found tugging at its mooring in a gentle breeze, but there was an eerie quiet around the seaplane ramp. Not a soul could be found who had any connection with the old flying boat. I became aware that something smelled riper than Jamaica Bay at low tide.

Luckily I had a pocketful of nickels to invest in the Bell Telephone Company. The haggling began, and I quickly discovered the seaplane rental had swollen to twice the original price tag.

My friend who had talked me into this unfortunate situation had good intentions. But even the best of intentions can be overridden by an unexpected opportunity to make a killing. His colleagues had got wind of my predicament, and were applying the heat.

It would have been unsafe to leave the shelter of my sweltering phone booth before a usable airplane could be found. My forty guests were either milling impatiently around the ramp or squatting menacingly on their toolboxes. Certainly my carcass would be thrown to the sharks if that flying boat stayed anchored at its mooring.

Suddenly the flow of nickels produced a glimmer of hope. NC58021 was hurrying northward from the Caribbean and would be in New York before sundown. If it could be coaxed to leave town again quickly, I might somehow survive this ordeal.

The battered telephone gulped its last nickel, and I emerged from my steaming refuge to face the music, but still with a trick or two left in my bag. I had been case-hardened for years in the airline crucible, and airplane delays were an old, familiar problem. Sometimes they must be played by ear.

Certainly this was not a suitable moment to soften up and confess that my embryonic airline had no real claim on any airplane, not even a rented one. This discrepancy would need to be soft-pedaled. For the moment the best technique was to herd my unhappy flock toward a restaurant where they could be plied with food and beverages. I located a suitable spot near La Guardia Airport, which had become the most likely point of departure.

But I soon discovered that NC58021 was not altogether a sure thing. For various legalistic reasons involving a government regulation that became effective at midnight, it would need to take off before the clock struck twelve, or not go at all until a complex airplane modification had been completed. If the airplane couldn't be dispatched quickly, the resulting delay would probably see the demise of Associated Air Transport, Inc., not to mention its chief executive.

The airplane needed some routine maintenance, and it would be a battle with the clock to make the midnight deadline. The mechanics seemed to be working in slow motion, but the minute hand of my wrist watch raced pell-mell around the dial. But finally everything was ready, and the passengers were boarded as fast as we could crowd them up the stairway. I was about to experience my first moment of peace since this hectic day began.

But it was not to be—at least not yet. Doctor Cox's elderly Aunt Reba had arrived on the scene. This lady of three score and ten was a bristling bundle of determined and militant energy, and she was fiercely protective of her nephew's interests. I greeted this formidable woman nervously, wondering why she had come at such an hour of the night. I knew no love was lost between Aunt Reba and the captain of NC58021, and he was standing beside me.

Aunt Reba's intentions were quickly unveiled. She announced she was going to Iceland and Stockholm as Doctor Cox's company inspector. A chill went up my spine.

The captain froze in his tracks. Bristling ominously he threatened to quit. So did my heart. Time was running out. The clock said it was ten minutes to the deadline.

Tempers got out of hand. Standing there between the obstinate Aunt Reba and the unyielding captain I felt like a referee when his fighters no longer obey his signals. But I had one trump card left to play. I could fly the airplane to Stockholm myself. I had a scheduled airline flight to London the next afternoon, but that could be rearranged if absolutely necessary.

At my wit's end I made the threat. The bedlam subsided. The decision went to Aunt Reba and she stomped triumphantly aboard the airplane at five minutes to midnight.

The door was slammed shut. The steps were pulled away. The four engines sputtered into action, and then settled down to play sweet music at an even tempo. The chocks were yanked swiftly, and all hands scattered for home. It was twelve o'clock midnight.

I waited on the deserted apron to watch the DC-4 taxi down the strip until only its lights were visible. After pausing briefly at the end of the runway the lights lifted gently into a starless sky, then disappeared into the night. NC58021 was on its way to Iceland and Stockholm.

The new company had cleared its highest hurdle, but its chief executive had suddenly grown older and wiser, and he felt lucky not to be draped in that telephone booth at the bottom of Jamaica Bay.

This, of course, was not the best way to run an airline or to maintain good health and sanity. If my company was going to stay in the air transportation business, it would be necessary to find an airplane, at least a rented one.

The bankroll had grown, but there still wasn't enough money for anything more ambitious than a lease. This problem was solved by a five-year-old flying boat. It was one of the two remaining Sikorsky S-44s—a sister ship of *Excalibur*. Although its hull was still young, and heavy with transatlantic glamor, this great ship had been cast aside in the postwar scramble for landplanes. But it served to rescue me, and I rescued it, too, by fishing it out of the aviation boneyard.

I had flown this airplane across the north and south Atlantic a great many times, enough to know every rivet in its graceful hull. Only a few months before, while on vacation, I had flown it south to Montevideo to look into the possibility of setting up a transatlantic airline to fly the flag of Uruguay.

The other of the two S-44s was still in Montevideo, but it had digressed from the original reason for being there. It was now involved with the rebels who were fighting the government of Paraguay, carrying supplies out of Montevideo in support of the rebellious forces.

I took delivery of the S-44 in Baltimore, and within a few hours the new black lettering on its gleaming skin proclaimed "Associated Air Transport." For good measure the flying boat was christened *Reykjavik*, in deference to the Icelandic capital which was the main hinge of the new airline.

This silvery beauty of a flying boat was ideally suited to our special needs. Among other things I no longer needed to worry about the unpredictable temperament of the captain of NC58021. I planned to do the flying myself between regular airline flights to London.

I could now eliminate the train ride from Minneapolis to New York and plan every flight direct from Minneapolis to Iceland, with a fuel stop in Newfoundland. There was plenty of water in the environs of Minneapolis to accommodate any-size flying boat. The fabled waters of Lake Minnetonka lapped very close to the city, making an excellent ready-made air terminal, which we made official by anchoring a mooring in a convenient cove.

The Sikorsky splashed down on Lake Minnetonka almost before the ink had dried on the airplane rental agree-

ment, and in doing so bugged the eyes of the summer va-
cationists who never thought such a sea-going monster
could stray so far from its ocean domicile.

On the first flight out of Lake Minnetonka we carried an
unusual group of passengers, of which a few looked as
though they might have escaped from the local jail. It appeared that their fear of the air had forced some of these
delicate souls to the overconsumption of spirits.

Getting these inebriated gentlemen into the unsteady
shoreboat and then disembarking them onto the flying boat
was a hazardous affair. But not a soul was lost, although
some did get wet. We eventually got everyone safely
aboard, with the difficult ones stowed in the rear passenger compartment where they were segregated from the
sober passengers.

But peace was short-lived. Soon after takeoff my be-
deviled and exasperated purser, Mario Borges, came scram-
bling up the ladder onto the flight deck to advise that
pandemonium was running rampant in the rear compartment over the possession of some whiskey bottles which had
been sneaked aboard.

I decided the best course of action would be to climb
to twelve thousand feet, where the shortage of oxygen in
the Sikorsky's unpressurized cabin would further addle the
intellects of my unruly customers and render them reasonably docile. After reaching this altitude I proceeded aft to
separate these passengers from the source of their problem.
In the rear compartment I found a half-dozen shirtless
gorillas entwined among each other like a mass of snakes,
wrestling listlessly for their beloved bottles.

I had no difficulty digging the offending spirits out
from under this pile of wriggling sweating humanity. Whatever strength they once possessed had been reduced to
total flabbiness by oxygen starvation. A stern warning even
caused them to fasten their seat belts like obedient children.

However, considering the total of three hundred passengers we eventually hauled to Iceland, the troublesome types were a tiny minority. Most of our passengers were skilled artisans from the twin cities who would be making a solid contribution to North Atlantic aviation.

After eighteen hundred miles of wilderness we dropped down into a long slash in the hilly Newfoundland forest for a landing on Gander Lake where an old friend of the flying boat days, Hugh Lacey, was waiting in a rowboat. He quickly secured a line to our stern and tailed us toward the dock where we could refuel for the ocean leg to Iceland.

The facilities at Reykjavik in Iceland were less quaint. We were assisted by a red-headed Scot who patrolled the harbor with a government-owned seaplane tender, a swift launch that lent dignity to the proceedings, together with an extra measure of safety when we arrived at night. His Very pistol fired warning shells to mark the position of unlighted channel buoys which could trouble us while landing in the dark.

The long summer twilight in the north allowed a high percentage of daylight flying, but our indiscriminate schedule often caused us to arrive or depart on the blackest of nights at Gander Lake, Reykjavik, and Stockholm. On a lake north of Stockholm the Swedish navy gave us a helping hand, but night-flying facilities for flying boats had vanished at every other port of call.

The sister ship of our airplane—the S-44 left behind in Montevideo—fell victim to this night-flying deficiency later in the summer. After failing to effect a daylight rendezvous with rebel gunboats on the Paraguay River, it returned to Montevideo after dark, still heavily burdened with its load of supplies. The pilot, who had a shortage of seaplane experience at night, attempted to land on the black, glassy waters of the River Plata without the aid of waterborne lights for guidance. Failing to level off, the big flying boat went to the bottom of the broad river to join the scuttled German battleship *Graf Spee* close by. The only crewman to survive this plunge was the flight engineer, Ken Dineen, who paddled aft through a break in the hull to eventually arrive at the surface, after which he spent a couple of weeks in the hospital.

Up on the North Atlantic we had no such drastic difficulty. Assisted by a pair of copilots, two flight engineers, and a steward, I finished off the Iceland contract ahead of schedule. But it added up to a lot of flying, and I averaged eleven airborne hours each day for thirty consecutive days. A pair of plush berths in the passenger cabin took the edge off the fatigue problem.

The heavily loaded takeoffs during the hot summer afternoons at Lake Minnetonka were a seagoing spectacle. On these hot days, above sea level and with less buoyancy than in salt water, the boat plowed through the water for hundreds of yards like a submarine before it could be coaxed onto the step to start its two mile run before lift-off.

A month of this sort of activity, embellished by a pair of unexpected westbound payloads from Stockholm and Reykjavik, turned out to be enough to forge the nugget that would finance my P-51 in the Arctic. But this adventure was still several years away, and meanwhile that nugget would be given other things to do.

CHAPTER SIX

The Tramp

The gold in my company's treasury jingled loudly enough to invite a large number of bright ideas on how to spend it. Therefore my affluence was short-lived.

A Miami company named Skyways International, which owned the Sikorsky flying boat I leased for the Iceland venture, had urgent need for a second C-46 Curtiss Commando to match the one it already had. The C-46 was a twin-engine transport twice the size of the better-known DC-3.

The acquisition of a second C-46 would allow Skyways to expand their lucrative transatlantic and Middle Eastern business. If I could find such an airplane to lease to them I could share in their international gold mine. In 1947 there were only seven commercially licensed C-46s in existence out of the hundreds built to fly as military transports during the war. Because a commercial version of this airplane was a rare gem, it seemed a wise move to gamble my small company treasury by converting a military model to civil license.

Hundreds of war-painted C-46s were sprawled out on war-surplus dumping grounds, mostly at remote airports that weren't used for much of anything else. All an American citizen needed to take full possession of a slightly used and remarkable transport was to part company with five thousand dollars before flying majestically away in the best airplane he could find in the parking lot. This big transport had originally cost Uncle Sam a quarter of a million dollars.

Such windfalls often come to grief on unpredictable snags, but this one surely couldn't miss. The only visible problem was the price tag for converting one of these military models to civil license under United States registry. This innocent-looking item cost nine times the price of the airplane itself.

Although the conversion cost was an unpleasant feature, because nine times five thousand was more than I had, there was plenty of mortgage money around to make up the difference. Therefore I climbed happily aboard the barrel and headed for the brink of the falls. It promised to be a soft landing because the Skyways lease guaranteed at least six thousand dollars each month in rental revenue.

A remote airport known as Walnut Ridge in the Midwest yielded a likely specimen of C-46 which was sorted out of a big flock by a young mechanical genius named Bill Lageman. Lageman stalked the moldering ghosts at Walnut Ridge until he found what he was looking for. This would be *Excalibur II*, although the name would never be formally proclaimed in any burst of champagne.

While *Excalibur II* was being modified for its license we digressed from the normal C-46 scheme of things by adding an extra fuel tank. This was a two-hundred-gallon monstrosity which reposed in the center of the big passenger and freight cabin like an oversize coffin. Although this ugly adornment further confused the hit-or-miss décor of bucket seats, life jackets, and life rafts that cluttered the cabin, there would be occasions when this extra fuel would be more than a bargain. In fact, before the year 1948 came to an end it would save the airplane from a wintry demise in the Labrador wilderness. Moreover, the extra fuel gave us a competitive edge over the other C-46 operators by adding several hundred miles to the range of the airplane. This extra flying range would eventually spell the difference between staying solvent and becoming financially embarrassed.

The extra fuel even made the C-46 into an authentic transatlantic airplane. Skyways took delivery of our ship on the first day of January of 1948 and started flying the Atlantic as if there were four engines instead of two. It took the long stride from Gander to Iceland or to the Azores, with plenty of fuel to spare.

When eastbound the new *Excalibur* carried freight— either medicine for Iran or tools for the oil rigs of Saudi Arabia. Westbound it disembarked refugees at Caracas on the north coast of Venezuela before heading home for Miami where it would be shaped up for its next round robin. This maintenance check came due after a hundred-flying-hour circuit that touched down on five continents.

The best feature of this pleasant and profitable arrangement was that I had no operational headaches. Skyways met the payroll, bought the fuel, performed the maintenance, and rustled up the payloads. I paid for the insurance and furnished the engines for the eventual periodic changes. The rest of the money went into the cash register, and I hoped this arrangement would go on forever.

In fact, the flow of gold was so stimulating that I brought another C-46 back from Walnut Ridge and committed it to the modification factory at Niagara Falls. I conjured fanciful dreams of a large fleet of airplanes, each one paying the bills for the next one coming along the conversion line. Leasing airplanes to young beavers who were eager to do the hard work of running an airline was certainly a fine technique for making money.

This was an aviation Utopia, but there was a black cloud gathering on the golden horizon. Rumors were thickening that a large fleet of the latest model C-46, a model which required no expensive conversion to get its civil license, would soon be available for lease from the federal government at a very cheap price. If these rumors were true I was climbing a long way out on a very fragile limb.

The rumors were accurate, and the limb suddenly broke. The Air Force, eager to have its mothballed fleet of late model C-46s flown by civilian operators to keep the airplanes in ready reserve status, began leasing C-46s by the dozen to a horde of would-be competitors, and to my client as well for a give-away rental fee of three hundred dollars per month. This was one-twentieth of the free market rate.

I scrambled for fiscal safety, leaving behind the latest C-46 acquisition from Walnut Ridge which was almost given away for fear it would eat us alive. Suddenly I had become the hard-pressed landlord of one white elephant instead of the opulent owner of two gold-coining flying machines. Skyways, naturally, ran for the exit, dropping our C-46 as if it were red-hot.

Excalibur II not only threatened to destroy what was left of last summer's hard-earned nugget, it also threatened personal ruin to the lone stockholder of the company. My name was formally inscribed on my airplane's man-sized mortgage, which called for a fifteen-hundred-dollar payment each month for a long time to come. This was five times what my competitors paid for renting an airplane from the federal government. Moreover, my insurance payments were twice what the government required of my competition.

Those rocks below the falls were pretty rough, and it didn't help much to curse the federals in Washington. Government agencies are habitually deaf to the yelps of a mere individual who happens to be unlucky enough to get mangled in the big government wringer.

The best course of action was to eat a little crow and take over all those tedious chores I had been freed of doing by leasing out the airplane, such as meeting the payroll, attending to the maintenance, buying the fuel, and drumming up business.

But my luck wasn't all bad. We were soon blessed with a nonscheduled operating certificate, granted by the Civil Aeronautics Administration, and earned the distinction of becoming a "supplemental" carrier.

Armed with this important piece of paper we leaped into a snake pit of uninhibited competition. Luckily my company presented a compact team that showed hardly an ounce of fatty overhead. Gordon Marsters was the entire ground staff. Dick Arms and Orville Bishop did the flying, with assistance from part-time copilots. Joe Nemeroff, the maintenance department, was also airborne part of the time. My job was to hold the financial bag, although my meal ticket was still my flying assignment with American Overseas Airlines.

The "supplemental" pickings turned out to be a starvation diet at this stage of nonscheduled airline development. Too many of the flood of new operators showed an instinct for the other fellow's jugular in the mad struggle to stay fiscally alive. The flooding of the market with ultra-cheap C-46s put normal free enterprise to rout. Every deal that came along paid little more than the fuel bills and salaries.

Marsters, who sought out the available market, grabbed any authentic business that would help pay the stack of bills, but there was nothing available that yielded a profit. Worse yet, we sometimes didn't collect the whole tab. For example, we had a contract at a hundred dollars a flying hour to carry a total of forty tons of freshly killed beef from Managua, Nicaragua, to Havana, Cuba. The first four of six trips were paid for promptly to lure us into flying the last two trips on credit. The middleman then grabbed the loot and was never seen again.

Nor was this meager contract easy to fulfill. Each trip started out from Miami with a load of innocent-looking boxes addressed to General Somoza, the strong-man dictator of Nicaragua. The boxes were labeled medicine, probably a special brand designed to doctor the political opposition.

At Managua a herd of cattle was observed grazing placidly on the airport meadow. But not for long. The peaceful, pastoral scene was quickly transformed into an orgy of blood and butchery. The cattle were slain where they grazed. Their dripping carcasses were weighed on scales that had been tampered with, and then piled aboard *Excalibur II* for the journey to Havana. These carcasses, incidentally, were also the property of the affluent General Somoza.

The airplane, dangerously overloaded because of those deceitful scales, its cabin awash with blood which oozed from every crack and crevice, just barely cleared the trees after using every inch of runway. To keep this overload of blood and beef in the air, the engines pounded at maximum power across mountains and jungle. It was only after reaching the sea that the overworked engines were throttled back slightly for the remainder of the journey to Havana. On the next trip the pilots brought along their own weighing apparatus.

The route from San Juan to New York, carrying swarms of Puerto Ricans, turned out to be our most reliable source of revenue. At forty dollars per passenger, minus an ambiguous fee to an ambiguous travel agent, this operation showed a small profit, even though it was flown almost empty on the southbound leg. On one occasion *Excalibur II* landed at its destination with one more passenger than it had when it took off. The new mother, totally unconcerned with the absence of privacy, gave birth atop the cabin fuel tank. A young Puerto Rican nurse who was a passenger on the flight took charge of the event, with Captain Orville Bishop reluctantly taking turns with his copilot as her assistant. Since the airplane had no galley, he patiently heated water over the flame of his cigarette lighter whenever it was needed. The baby girl was promptly named Orvilla in honor of the bashful and embarrassed captain, to the fascinated delight of an amphitheaterful of sympathetic passengers, and in spite of the howling protests of the new arrival.

Although business was otherwise scarce, my home telephone never stopped jangling with a multitude of prospective deals that seldom bore fruit. The C-46 did carry a load of horses to Santiago in the Chilean south latitudes, and a crew of Finnish seamen from Pori, Finland, to Jacksonville, Florida. We also quoted prices on shipments of gold to Tangier, Madagascar, and other faraway places, but these exotic gold-transfer deals somehow never quite worked out.

Our bread-and-butter flying out of San Juan was persistent and frequent, and the profit margin, though modest, was enough to convince me we ought to stay on this route. Our airplane, with its extra fuel tank, was especially suited to the direct sixteen hundred and twenty-five mile nonstop flight from San Juan to New York, while our C-46 competition flew hundreds of extra miles for an en route fuel stop at Miami.

However, almost everyone in the company was itching for a change of scenery, and because I wanted to keep my excellent staff in a good frame of mind, I eventually succumbed to their pressure for a fling on the continent of Europe.

In the aftermath of World War II there were severe adjustments being made on this badly bruised continent. The refugee camps were overflowing with hundreds of thousands of the homeless and stateless who were eager to reach Palestine, despite the bitter war that was being fought in their promised land. The refugee agencies were searching for inexpensive air transportation to bridge the miles between Europe and the new nation in the Middle East.

Because economical air transportation was our specialty, I poked around the back streets of London to sound out an African air charter company which did business in Palestine. This outfit was eager to charter a big airplane, complete with a staff of flying personnel, to do a job where their own smaller DC-3s fell short. So we were engaged to fly refugees out of Munich to Haifa.

But there was one reservation. I was not in favor of letting my C-46 fly passengers across the Alps and the Adriatic in severe mid-winter weather on two heavily burdened engines, knowing that one engine would not suffice for a great distance if the other failed. Radio facilities and usable landing strips were almost nonexistent between Munich and Haifa on the direct route to Palestine. Therefore I insisted on a safe sea-level alternate route around the mountains by way of Marseilles and the Mediterranean to be used whenever the weather required it.

This important detail was finally included in the contract, but our client, for reasons of his own, decided to shift the point of departure from Munich to Marseilles.

This move generated another kind of trouble. France, unlike Germany at this time, was a sovereign nation with complete control of all payloads originating at its airports. Marseilles should have been used only as a refueling stop.

I raised a questioning eyebrow when asked to set up headquarters in Marseilles, but to no avail. Because we couldn't afford to bicker and delay I dispatched the C-46 into this French port with everything and everybody we had, including an extra flight crew and a spare engine.

The French, as I expected, were not elated about playing host to an American airplane doing a Mediterranean business out of a French port. Still, seven quick trips were flown out of Marseilles before the curtain fell. In the course of these seven trips we managed to transfer three hundred and fifty forlorn souls from Europe's refugee camps into war-gripped Haifa.

To avoid legal complications that were likely to develop out of the jabbering confusion at Marseilles following the shutdown, I hustled *Excalibur II* to safe sanctuary in Geneva. The airplane left France with such haste that the spare engine was left behind, never to be seen again. Somewhere in the background someone was applying the heat, trying to force us into flying from Munich through the Alps in all kinds of weather.

Having found haven in Switzerland we optimistically expected that the airplane would soon be pressed into service at Munich on the contract terms. Meanwhile, our nonchalant competitors were blithely flying their C-46s across the Alps in the heaviest weather, indifferent to the possibility of the failure of an engine.

We were advised that our C-46 would be welcome in Munich if we would let it do what everyone else was doing and if, in spite of the contract, we would pay our own costs for the unplanned sojourn in Geneva. Convinced that our contract was valid, and that we were right, we refused and held out in our Alpine sanctuary.

With our costs running in the thousands of dollars each week, the entire company sat immobilized in Switzerland for six weeks, waiting for the call that never came. Finally the attrition of dollars caused an economic retreat to the western side of the Atlantic, where we could regain our fiscal health on the less glamorous route from San Juan to New York.

Excalibur II, first on the refugee scene, had the inside track to the Middle East. There was significant wealth at the far end, but the track wasn't clear.

I was momentarily dismayed by the setback, but there

is a sense of fulfillment sometimes which transcends the profit motive. In the long view of history *Excalibur*'s role in the great exodus was all to the good. This battered tramp of the airways did a good turn. Three hundred and fifty unlucky people found a new lease on life in their promised land, and they flew there with an extra factor of safety.

We had our share of better luck, too. Our C-46 always enjoyed the best of mechanical health. On the two occasions during its career when it suffered a failed engine, there was a spare immediately on hand. When a Miami hurricane blew its rudder askew, the airplane was back in service within twenty-four hours.

But this faithful workhorse failed to make a significant profit in a risky environment. It merely circulated the currency. Therefore it was put up for sale, to be delivered after the company personnel found something else to do.

My C-46 finally found a new flag and moved a long way south to new horizons. It was a bargain for a Bolivian outfit which used it to haul freshly killed beef from the valley of Cochabamba to the high plateau of La Paz.

But its luck in South America eventually took a bad turn. On a routine takeoff at thirteen thousand five hundred feet from the lofty airport at La Paz, the thin air of the high plateau conspired with a tired engine to prevent the airplane from getting safely airborne. It failed to clear the ridge and was smashed to oblivion on an insignificant outcropping of the mighty Andes. But *Excalibur II*'s safety slate was still clean. Everyone scrambled safely from the wreckage.

CHAPTER SEVEN

Off Airways

The Iceland nugget was still intact but a little frazzled by all the wear and tear it suffered while keeping *Excalibur II* airborne. It grew no bigger, but its owner gained a lot of experience.

The next airplane would surely be noncommercial. There were interesting things to be done with airborne vehicles besides making a lot of money. For instance, could there be anything better than a single-engine fighter or a racing airplane for escaping earthbound realities and, among other things, recapturing my transatlantic speed record?

Even back in the mid-thirties I was intrigued with setting speed records. In those days Benny Howard's *Mister Mulligan* was on top of the heap in the Bendix transcontinental races. *Mulligan* didn't have the sleek lines of a racing airplane. It was a high-wing monoplane with fixed landing gear, but it was a great performer in its day, and possessed the potential for doing a lot more than it ever did. Moreover, at that particular time the airline strategists were beginning to think heavily about flying above the weather, rather than through it. Tommy Tomlinson of TWA was probing the upper troposphere in his single-engine Northrup in an effort to prove that the airways of the future would be high in the upper atmosphere.

Mulligan, it seemed to me, could do the same job better, and collect a few records at the same time. All it needed was a special kind of supercharger to make it fly higher and faster than it was accustomed to go.

There happened to be just the right device to fit *Mulligan*'s engine, and it was the only one of its kind. This was the two-stage supercharger used by Wiley Post in the *Winnie Mae* during his high-altitude transcontinental flights a couple of years before.

If the *Winnie Mae* could be blown along at three hundred and forty miles an hour while flying above thirty thousand feet between Los Angeles and Cleveland, then *Mulligan* could average at least a mile a minute faster— four hundred miles an hour—on a nonstop transcontinental flight with a similar tailwind. Certainly a six-hour coast-to-coast record in the year 1937 would help settle the argument for flying higher and faster.

The Eclipse-Pioneer Company thought enough of the idea to lend me the *Winnie Mae*'s supercharger. The only missing ingredient was the airplane.

This turned out to be an insurmountable snag. *Mulligan*'s new variable-pitch propeller lost a blade over New Mexico during the annual Bendix race, and that was the end of *Mulligan,* the only one of its kind. This crack-up almost saw the end of Benny Howard, too, but, possessing nine lives like a cat, Benny pulled through.

It would have cost a lot of money to put the airplane back together, and there just wasn't enough available.

Therefore, the high-altitude supercharger was put back in storage, and the high-speed dream just faded away.

Another brainstorm came along a few years later. I developed a crush on Frank Fuller's Seversky P-35 pursuit plane, which was the forerunner of the famous Republic P-47 Thunderbolt. The P-35 was another Bendix-race winner under the guidance of Fuller. But the money problem was the stumbling block again, so I never even came close to the glamorous P-35.

I didn't give up, but more than a decade passed before an airplane, an idea and the necessary cash got together all at the same time. Finally, in January of 1950, my C-46, *Excalibur II*, left a bundle of money in the wake of its sale, and a new idea came along to fit the size of my bankroll. At the same time I met a pair of aviators named Paul.

Paul Penrose, a wartime P-51 test pilot, was a specialist at racing the P-51. After quizzing him for hours, I discovered that this airplane was an aviator's dream. Paul Mantz, who owned and flew a pair of his own racing P-51s, was willing to sell one.

So I bought his N1202, an airplane that had already made a record for itself. It was the winner of the Bendix race from Los Angeles to Cleveland in 1946 and 1947. It placed second in 1948, third in 1949.

This airplane, together with its Rolls-Royce engine, was a remarkable combination that could do better than win a race. I was convinced that it could set a new record for a flight around the world solo, a mark which stood at seventy-three hours, and take back the Atlantic speed record on the first leg.

Therefore I added some extra fuel capacity to a wing which already carried twice as much as it was designed for, and installed the latest and strongest model of the Rolls-Royce Merlin, an engine which could deliver its maximum continuous power all the way up to thirty-five thousand feet. The cockpit was unpressurized, so in addition I built in a sixteen-hour oxygen supply. I wasn't looking forward to wearing an oxygen mask for hours at a stretch, but it was all that was needed in the unpressurized cockpit as long as I paid careful heed to its proper use.

A look at the globe sufficed to determine the route and the fuel stops. After leaving New York the first landing would be in London, thirty-five hundred miles away. The next stop would be at Baghdad, then Calcutta, Tokyo, Anchorage, and back to New York. Pan American Airways would expedite the P-51 through the fuel stops. Even though I was still flying for American Overseas Airlines, we were about to merge with Pan American.

Fifty-four hours of elapsed time from New York to New York would be a tight but reasonable schedule for the journey. By gently flogging the engine, I could make the P-51 cruise at a true airspeed of four hundred miles an hour without protest. This respectable airspeed, plus a few knots of tailwind, plus five fuel stops expending one hour each, added up to a flight plan of two days and six hours—nineteen hours better than the existing record.

The main problem would be fatigue. There could never be any real substitute for sleep, but there was a partial remedy. Bill Lear offered to contribute an automatic pilot, and Paul Penrose suggested a device that would ring an alarm when the rate of oxygen flow indicated something was amiss with the breathing schedule. As long as the oxygen reached my lungs, the discomforts of the undersize cockpit and the seat-pack parachute would assure that my catnaps would be suitably short. The P-51's cruising altitude would be miles above all other traffic, thus making sure it would not be a dangerous derelict of the airways during my less alert moments. On top of that I developed a capacity for going long periods without sleep.

It was easy enough to get clearances to cross the numerous nations along the route. Red China was the only outfit not consulted, but it would be traversed at night. There was little chance my trusty Rolls-Royce would let me fall into this inhospitable territory. Certainly the Red Chinese Air Force could do nothing about a high-flying P-51 during the hours of darkness.

My airline had given the proposed journey a reluctant go-ahead. After a few more shakedown flights everything would be ready for circumnavigating the planet. Nothing appeared to stand in the way.

But on June 25, 1950, the North Koreans changed the course of American affairs, and mine along with them.

I was westbound out of London on a peaceful June Sunday when the news of the invasion of South Korea reached the flight deck of my Stratocruiser. It took only a couple of minutes of listening to realize that my round-the-world plans had been shot down in the flames of war. Round-the-world flights would be decidedly unwelcome in the new international atmosphere. In peacetime such a trip would have been hailed as an achievement. In time of war the flight would appear frivolous.

It took a few weeks to recover from this jolt and decide on a useful alternative. The more normal P-51s (lately called F-51s) were in the thick of the fighting in Korea. But what could an old fighter airplane without guns hope to contribute?

A new idea that might have military value eventually unfolded, but it would take some additional preparation. A gunless P-51 with four thousand miles of flying range might point in the direction of new reconnaissance concepts, and there could be nothing much better than the Arctic for proving the navigational aspects. Therefore, I started practicing in the direction of Alaska.

Nothing went right on this shakedown flight to the Arctic Circle, but it showed me every fault of my airplane. Any future trip was likely to be easy by comparison.

This P-51, because of its many modifications, carried an experimental license that specified it must stay clear of populated areas. Of these modifications, the most significant was the "wet" wing. Fuel was simply poured into the interior of the wing, which was liberally treated inside with zinc chromate paste to minimize the leaks. Fuel pumps were installed at low points in the wing structure to assure uninterrupted flow of fuel to the engine, and to make sure all the fuel in the wing would be usable—all six hundred and ninety gallons of the total of eight hundred and sixty-five in the airplane.

The designer of the P-51 did not have this arrangement in mind when he conceived the airplane. Therefore it was reasonable to expect some difficulty. While flying at high altitude from Los Angeles toward Alaska I became aware of the problems wrought by the extensive wing modifications. Though I was fully aware of the fuel leaks *under* the wing, I wasn't expecting any leakage out of the *top*, which proved to be so porous along the rivet lines that a fine mist of high octane gasoline exuded the entire length of the upper wing surface.

This was an unpleasant development which would certainly need fixing. To make matters even more uncomfortable the engine surged noisily because it was not getting a smooth flow of fuel at high altitude; this caused me to suspect an inadequate fuel pump. The rumbling and grumbling of the fuel-hungry Rolls-Royce, together with the menacing cloud of gasoline vapor suggested it might be better to fly to Alaska some other day.

While thinking this over I dropped a few thousand feet lower to discover that the heavier atmosphere helped smooth the regurgitations of the engine. Moreover, having burned off some of the fuel, the spray of gasoline vapor seemed to have disappeared. Still, I resolved to steer clear of any kind of atmospheric electricity.

I was learning the whims of my odd airplane, but it still seemed wise to get back on the ground to think things over. Therefore, I dropped into Seattle to get an earthbound perspective and a chance to stretch out the kinks that plagued my long legs in the P-51's cramped cockpit.

A night of refreshing sleep brought on a new spurt of optimism, enough to see me northbound again on the airway to Alaska. If my plans for this airplane were to bear fruit, it would be important to have a look at the approaches to Fairbanks.

The Fairbanks reconnaissance was completed, but there was no time left over for loitering on the Arctic Circle. My next airline schedule out of New York to London was only a couple of days away.

After overnighting in the city of Fairbanks I returned to the airplane the following morning to find rivulets of gasoline streaming along the bottom of the wing, coursing through the loop housing of the automatic direction finders on the bottom of the fuselage. A measurement of the tanks showed that a hundred and fifty expensive gallons of high octane had drained off during the night.

The fuel leakage had reached disturbing proportions, but I could hardly leave my twenty-five thousand dollar investment in Fairbanks on Air Force real estate. Some hard-headed bureaucrat might condemn the ailing airplane and bulldoze it into scrap metal. Furthermore there was no airline in Fairbanks which could fly me back to New York in time for my flight schedule to London.

I felt that the least of my problems was the leak, so I decided to fly my leaking P-51 back to Burbank, where it could be fixed and where I could find a fast ride to New York. It was twenty-nine hundred miles to Los Angeles —approximately eight flying hours if I poured on the coal.

The airplane was gassed for the second time, and a fair-sized crowd gathered to watch the takeoff, convinced they were about to witness a spectacle. But they were cheated. Nothing spectacular happened, and I was soon at thirty-five thousand feet over Whitehorse in the Yukon, struggling to stay on top of a frontal cloud formation which was obviously alive with static electricity. I wasn't altogether successful, and each time my fuel-heavy airplane penetrated the cloud tops my apprehension grew. I didn't enjoy playing games with atmospheric electricity.

The stream of gasoline into the loop housing of the automatic direction finder had rendered my radio navigation equipment useless, except that I could still hear the aural signals of the radio ranges. However, it would be difficult to miss the entire west coast of the United States, so I pointed the P-51 in the general direction of California.

The engine ran more smoothly than the day before, but all of a sudden it ran completely dry and quit. This happened at night and the cockpit lights failed along with the engine. I didn't waste time groping around my cramped quarters for the flashlight. By instinct I went directly for the fuel valve and switched to another tank, which brought back the reassuring staccato. The engine quit a second time that night, but I was ready, flashlight in hand.

Los Angeles Airport was fogged in for the midnight arrival, but across the Hollywood Hills at Burbank the cloud ceiling was at a meager four hundred feet. A misty mile of visibility greeted the first nonstop flight from Fairbanks to Los Angeles.

But there was no other greeting. There might have been a warmer welcome if I had wired ahead to announce my impending arrival. Someone might have been around to help push the P-51 into its parking place. Being unannounced, I did all the pushing myself.

No record was either sought or claimed, although an eight-hour flight from Fairbanks to Los Angeles probably was the best at that time. But records were a minor consideration. The main objective was to find out if the P-51 could do what I wanted, and I found that it could.

The first step would be to fix my airplane. The next step would be to go after that Atlantic speed record.

CHAPTER EIGHT

Shakedown

Today is the day. Before January 31, 1951, is checked off the calendar, I should nail that Atlantic speed record back on my escutcheon.

Although today's flight is a final warm-up exercise for the journey I plan across the Arctic and the North Pole, my thoughts between New York and London will be riveted on speed.

My sleek and shiny P-51 fighter, *Excalibur III*, can take the record easily, with or without a tailwind. It would be especially soul-satisfying to put the blue ribbon high on the shelf for a while. A powerful tailwind will make the prize unreachable by any airplane until the jets come along.

Heaton Owsley, the wind expert at Pan Am, called to say, "Tonight's the night. It should average a hundred on the tail."

That broke up the bridge game.

The big wind of the westerlies is out there. I hope to find it and hitch a ride in the high-speed core of the North Atlantic jet stream.

This shakedown flight is scheduled to cover thirty-five hundred miles nonstop from New York to London, riding the rapids of this river in the sky. Although I have flown the same route hundreds of times in four-engine airliners, this is my first solo crossing. It is also my first with only one engine, and I'm planning to push along at maximum power all the way, as much as the engine will continuously deliver, without courting trouble.

One of the first people I meet at the airport is a Pan Am captain, Emory Martin. He has just brought a Stratocruiser in from Europe. I inquire about the winds.

"You've got 'em," he assures me.

Martin has been flying airliners almost since the airlines began. I take him out and show him my little airplane.

He doesn't talk much. It's too cold. He just says, "H'mm."

I feel a twinge of embarrassment. It doesn't seem too sensible to be taking a racing P-51 to London in the middle of the night.

I needn't have felt that way. Martin is the kind who would like to be going along.

My schedule calls for taking off at two-thirty in the morning, but the frigid blast of air pouring down into New York from Canada has temporarily frozen the valves on the fuel truck, causing a two-hour delay, and is freezing me, too. In the cold darkness before dawn at New York International Airport the prospect of a solo journey across the Atlantic is more bleak than it was at that high-spirited bridge game.

The fueling delay has caused other problems to magnify. The late takeoff will mean a late landing at London in darkness and fog, instead of a midafternoon arrival in good weather.

But months of planning and preparation have created a momentum which is not easy to arrest, and somewhere high over the ocean near the great-circle route there is a river of air rushing east, and I'm eager to ride its rapids. It'll take more than a frozen fuel truck or the London fog to cool off my plans.

The P-51 is finally gassed with eight hundred and sixty-five gallons of high octane and is ready to go. Bob Hixson, who forsook a warm night's sleep to give me a word of encouragement in the midst of this freezing blast, joins me in a final weather briefing which includes a fresh new folder of meteorological charts. It is these documents, a collection of ocean weather charts whose curving lines show atmospheric pressure and temperature at various levels up to thirty-five thousand feet, which predict the location of the big wind I'm gunning for—the North Atlantic jet stream.

The name "jet stream" is often supposed to be derived from the jet engine. But there's no connection, and it is mere coincidence that the weather men selected the word "jet" in their effort to describe a phenomenon they can't yet fully explain. For me it's sufficient to be familiar with these charts of highs, lows, isotherms, millibar surfaces, etc., which can tell me if, and just about where, the jet stream is blowing.

I climb aboard the P-51 and find the tiny cockpit a refuge against the bitter northeast wind. A mechanic helps jam me into my cramped quarters and closes the canopy lid. I discovered a long time ago that they built the Mustang for little guys.

The cockpit seems much smaller than it did yesterday when I ferried the airplane across the Hudson River from Teterboro. I'm now encased, among other things, in an extra layer of clothing. Underneath my ordinary business suit is an underwear garment of the long red kind, a concession to the deep-freeze of the stratosphere. A white shirt and subdued tie complete the ensemble, on top of which is a threadbare summer flying suit which I'll peel off before invading the lobby of the Savoy Hotel in London.

The cockpit accommodations are all the more torturous because of my seat-pack parachute and life jacket. The parachute harness fits so snugly over my life jacket and emergency oxygen bottle that the combination promises to be more of a strangulating hazard than a design for survival. My best precaution is a handy Boy Scout knife for stabbing the air out of the life jacket if it should accidentally inflate.

With my physical dimensions thus swollen by "life-saving" equipment it becomes more difficult than ever to even squirm in the cockpit. I contemplate discarding the disabling chute and life jacket, but am sure such a move would appear reckless. Just flying this contraption on a night like this looks bad enough.

In fact, the life jacket would only prolong the agony in the unlikely event of an ocean dunking. January, to be sure, is not the best month for North Atlantic bathing.

I decide to accept the extra hazard of being squeezed too tightly in this tiny cage. I've been taught that emergency equipment is sacrosanct, even if it kills instead of saves.

I am as ready to go as I ever will be. After a couple of tries the big Rolls-Royce engine starts sputtering and spitting in protest against the bitter cold. The control tower gives clearance to taxi and advises that a Port Authority station wagon will escort me out to the runway. Fighter aircraft are seldom allowed at New York's biggest airport, and require special arrangements.

While taxiing, there is no forward visibility behind the big engine, so the escorting vehicle proceeds alongside. We arrive at Runway Four. The driver waves a cordial farewell. I wonder for a moment if he thinks I'm crazy.

He probably does, and maybe I am.

The northeasterly surface wind is blowing a gusty twenty knots, and it leaves little doubt I'll be bucking a vigorous headwind halfway up to cruising altitude. I realize this will cost a few minutes, and while contemplating losing this precious time the cockpit lights flicker out, leaving me in total darkness. I mumble a curse or two, and fumble like a blind man for the flashlight.

I find it, and squirt the beam around the cockpit. The engine is still coughing an occasional protest. I close the radiator coolant shutter and it soon starts purring smoothly. While waiting I run through a memorized check list of the "kill" items before calling the control tower for the airways clearance. Because there is no other traffic the clearance snaps back immediately through the chill of the night: "ATC clears N-one-two-oh-two to London via Boston, Yarmouth, Sydney, Gander, great circle to St. Eval; cross Boston above fifteen thousand." I repeat the clearance to make sure there is no misunderstanding. As I sit here behind only one engine, St. Eval, near Land's End, England, seems so much farther away than it does when flying with four engines.

Actually I don't intend to fly via St. Eval at all. St. Eval is a weak radio beacon near Land's End and too easy to miss. On this particular ocean crossing I would like something more substantial to aim at, which means it will be better to fly a hundred miles farther north and pin down the powerful radio range at Shannon Airport in southwest Ireland. But the clearance can be revised later. There is no other high-altitude traffic flying the Atlantic.

The engine run-up is smooth, with hardly a drop of engine revolutions on either magneto. I clamp on the rubber face mask, and adjust it tightly across my nose and mouth to assure no oxygen leakage.

"Cleared for takeoff." The voice from the control tower calls for action. I thrust the throttle forward. My right hand is full of both control stick and flashlight. It is 0450 New York time, 0950 in London. The big four-bladed propeller flails lustily as the P-51 roars down the runway into the northeaster. At a hundred and forty-five miles an hour on the airspeed indicator the tires take leave of the New York concrete.

The wheels thump up into their sockets and I cruise low at the base of the overcast, gathering speed as the power of the thundering Rolls-Royce asserts itself. I wonder how much ice there might be between the bottom and the tops of these cold-soaked clouds. Suddenly the airplane is totally immersed in the murky mists, and the sharp staccato of snow pellets on the canopy suggests that I'd better climb as quickly as possible to the top of the weather. I shift the beam of the flashlight from the instrument panel to the darkness outside. It reveals a thin coating of frosty ice on the wing's leading edge, and *Excalibur III* has no deicers.

The P-51 wallows up through a mixture of sleet and snow while I concentrate on the instruments from behind the flashlight—"wallow," in fact, understates the gyration, but there's nothing I can do to stop it now. Until most of the fuel in the tank behind my seat is burned off, *Excalibur III* will porpoise instead of fly.

At twenty-three thousand feet I cut in the high blower for more engine supercharging of the thinning atmosphere. At twenty-five thousand feet the P-51 is on top of all clouds, and at twenty-nine thousand feet my little fighter is leveled off at the initial cruising altitude. I have no intention to cruise in the usual fuel-economizing sense. The throttle is thrust forward for maximum allowable engine power as specified by its manufacturer, and I intend to keep it that way.

The thin ridge of ice along the leading edge of the wing costs some airspeed. I glance back at the two radio antennas to check if an ice coating might have carried them away. They are still there and free of ice. The air is smooth and there should now be a quartering tailwind. We pass over Boston thirty-seven minutes from takeoff and head out over the Atlantic toward Yarmouth at the southern tip of Nova Scotia.

Forty minutes from Boston, Yarmouth goes by. My little airplane is doing a sluggish four hundred miles an hour groundspeed, but the airspeed is now improving slightly as the fuel load lightens, and the ice slowly evaporates from the wings. The coast of Nova Scotia is visible almost six miles below. A glow of twilight in the east kindles a new flame of optimism.

I stow the flashlight and shift the fuel-selector valve to the right-wing tank, leaving some forty gallons in the fuse-lage tank as an emergency reserve. The ship is now perfectly stable, with the elevator trim tab riding on zero of the indicator. Now that the fuel load is adjusted, there is no more tendency for the aircraft to wallow, and I can maneuver if necessary without fear of unpleasant consequences. I peer down at the coast of Nova Scotia which rolls underneath at increasing speed.

Halifax passes under the starboard wing, visible below scattered clouds. One hundred and thirty-seven miles in nineteen minutes is four hundred and thirty-two miles an hour. In view of the reduced drift angle, it appears that the wind at this altitude has backed around from northwest to west-northwest, giving more of a boost. The wind velocity exceeds a hundred miles an hour, and *Excalibur III* has been crabbing into it at a 15 degree angle to avoid being blown off course and out to sea.

It is now full daylight. I unfasten the seat belt and shoulder harness and start tinkering with the radio. Up to now I've been unable to adjust the receiver because of my awkward lighting arrangement, and have spoken with no one since leaving New York. I should have checked in with the Eastern Defense Command by radio, being aware that the Air Force has been tracking my P-51 with radar all the way up the coast. But now I'll wait to make my first ground contact with the airport control tower at Sydney, on the northeastern tip of Nova Scotia.

After setting up the radio transmitter and receiver, I switch on the oil transfer pump, which transfers oil from the ten-gallon reserve tank into the engine oil tank. The engine should be consuming slightly over a gallon of oil each hour, and the plan calls for transferring two gallons into the main oil supply at two-hour intervals. Since the transfer pump delivers a gallon a minute, it should be switched off in two minutes, but I forget to do so.

Six minutes later I remember the switch. Six gallons should have been transferred, but where did all that oil go?

Unless the engine has seriously overconsumed, the engine oil tank should have overflowed by several gallons. There should be oil all over the forward part of the cockpit canopy, but there's not a drop on it. Where *did* that oil go?*

I worry a little. If the engine has changed its habits and has burned more oil than is normal, I have a troublesome problem, particularly in view of that two thousand mile stretch of open ocean beyond Newfoundland. I resolve to keep a sharp eye on the oil pressure and temperature and to be careful to throttle back with the slightest change of the indicators. The engine has been delivering maximum power, twenty-seven hundred revolutions per minute and forty-six inches of manifold pressure, and I'm planning to use this high power throughout the journey unless the oil pressure falters.

The twin cities of Sydney and Glace Bay appear in miniature far below, and the broad reach of the Gulf of St. Lawrence lies ahead. I report over Sydney at twenty-nine thousand feet, two hours and one minute out of New York, and then follow the "on course" signal of the northeast leg of Sydney's radio range while heading across the

---

* It wasn't until after the trip was completed that I discovered that the oil transfer pump delivered oil much more slowly at high altitudes than the original calibration at sea level had indicated.

Gulf toward Newfoundland. The groundspeed has eased up to four hundred and fifty miles an hour.

As fuel is consumed from the right-wing tank, the ship becomes left-wing heavy. I try to use the aileron trim tab to compensate, but it's frozen tight. The outside air temperature is 50 degrees below zero. I shift the fuel selector to the left-wing tank so as to eventually regain lateral balance. Because of the frozen trim tab, it will now be necessary to shift the fuel selector more often to maintain reasonable trim. This procedure is going to complicate my bookkeeping of the fuel supply.

After crossing the Gulf of St. Lawrence the southwest leg of Gander's radio range becomes the guideline. Somewhere up ahead I should find the core of the jet stream.

The quartering tailwind is almost a hundred miles an hour, but I'm looking for a two-hundred-mile-an-hour specimen. My fast-moving airplane is closing in on Gander before I get some disheartening news.

"One-two-oh-two from Gander Tower. I have your met info. Are you ready to copy?"

"Fire away."

I jot down the numbers on my weather folder. It's a long message, but it doesn't take much of a brain to boil it down. The core of the jet is south of St. Johns instead of over Gander.

I've overshot the jet stream, and it's too late for a detour.

I feel depressed and strangely listless.

Had I started out across the ocean from St. Johns, to the southeast of Gander, we would be hustling along one hundred miles an hour faster in the strongest part of the big wind. As it has turned out I'll be waiting and hoping to hit the core of the jet stream out near the middle of the Atlantic where it should curve north again. It's out there, invisible and elusive. But without ground check points passing underneath to determine my actual speed, I can only grope for it with fingers crossed.

My movements in the cockpit and conversations with the Gander Control Tower seem to have drained away a lot of my strength. I don't understand it. Disappointment has never affected me this way before. I notice an odd, pungent odor within my oxygen mask and begin a fit of coughing which projects the mask away from my face.

The cockpit instruments become so dimly readable that the dials lose their meaning. Whooping into the thin air at twenty-nine thousand feet, my will to stay awake is ebbing away. The airplane flops aimlessly in the stratosphere, one wing going down, then up, then down, and then up, rocking me deeper into sleep. I'm on the verge of becoming a witless derelict in the Newfoundland sky, being blown out to sea on a torrent of wind.

Excalibur III plunges to twenty-five thousand feet before I can fight my way back to consciousness enough to ram the oxygen mask back on my face and hold it there so tightly that the precious flow can't escape. More by instinct than intention I flip the oxygen-flow lever to its emergency position which floods the mask with pure oxygen. This new breath of life probably saved the P-51 and its contents from disappearing altogether from the aviation scene.

The oxygen flow has started up my thinking processes again and I'm beginning to realize what happened. While twisting around in the cockpit and jotting down Gander's discouraging wind information, my mask had loosened and allowed the flow of oxygen to escape above the nose-piece, instead of finding its way into my lungs. This deficiency was especially full of danger because the P-51's tiny cabin is not pressurized. The air is as thin inside the cabin as outside, which calls for the most careful precautions and a close-fitting oxygen mask.

For an hour I sit perfectly still, refilling my lungs and concentrating with all my will power to stay awake and keep an eye on the little compass up in the bow of the canopy. At first my heavy-lidded eyes can barely see the 100 degree reading, but at the end of an hour I have regained my wits sufficiently to try to figure out what happened, especially in the navigation department.

If I held a good compass course during that subconscious hour, the navigation is okay. If not, I am somewhere over the Atlantic—*position unknown*—and must make the best of it. I have a blurred memory of passing over Gander at what should have been 1235 on the Greenwich clock, two hours and forty-five minutes out of New York, and thirty minutes behind the flight plan.

In the midst of the oxygen crisis I recall a vague glimpse of the runways at Gander as we blew by. The black runways, neatly etched in a blanket of snow, were almost too inviting to resist, considering the extent of my difficulty. I dimly remember thinking it might be a good idea to land there and try again another time, with all of today's uncertainties tidied up.

I must have rejected the thought because here I am, an hour later, probably five hundred miles out to sea. Unless the steering job was excessively wobbly during that hour of relapse there should be a position check up ahead in the vicinity of weather ship *Charlie*, a Coast Guard vessel stationed near the middle of the Atlantic, eight hundred and sixty miles out from Gander.

Excalibur III has the upper sky all to itself. Airline traffic in the year 1951 never exceeds twenty-five thousand feet. Having regained my health I decide to hustle back up to twenty-nine thousand feet with the hope of increasing the tailwind. I alter course ten degrees to starboard to maintain the great-circle track, and before long the automatic direction finder picks up the radio beacon on *Charlie*. It points directly over the nose. At least I know where we're heading. My luck is getting better.

We're closing fast on the weather ship. A coastguards-man is tracking the tiny P-51 blip on his radar. He passes me a couple of fixes.

"What kind of a machine have you got?" he inquires. "You're doing five hundred and twenty knots."

"A P-51," I answer, only half-realizing what he was saying. I don't feel like chatting about the airplane. All I care about is that elusive wind.

Suddenly his words sink in, but I'm not sure I heard correctly. Half-afraid to hear the answer I ask him to repeat the speed.

"Yeah," he says. "You're doing five hundred and twenty knots. We're not used to that." He continues on, "Must be lonesome up there in a P-51."

I don't answer. All I can think about is that five hundred twenty knots is *six hundred miles an hour*—I've found that big wind!

Out here in mid-ocean *Excalibur III* and I are riding that two-hundred-mile-an-hour tailwind we've been searching for.

This is a strange speed run. Over a featureless ocean nothing appears to move much. The airplane seems to hang motionless in the air. The thrill of speed comes only in the numbers the radarman has passed along.

I have been riding, or bucking, jet streams for years on scheduled flights, but this is the first time I've deliberately sought one out to check the theory of the weatherman.

Over the years, out of the mass of radiosonde and high-altitude data collected during World War II have come theories of intensification of the prevailing temperate-zone westerlies that are part of the global pattern. In attempts to check these ideas, north-south vertical slices of North American sky were mapped with points of equal westwind velocity joined by lines. There, on paper, visible for the first time at a bullseye of concentric circles of increasing speed, was the concentrated high-speed flow that has earned the name "jet stream."

Although it appears round on the meteorological charts which, for convenience, are much squeezed in breadth and exaggerated in height, the core of the jet stream is a flat river of air, fifty to one hundred miles wide and several miles thick. It flows usually at altitudes from four to nine miles, and can reach velocities in excess of three hundred miles an hour.

It doesn't stay put. Seldom straight, it meanders around the entire northern hemisphere, moving south or north with the location of the cold air "polar front" and being frequently broken at various points. It strengthens in winter, weakens in summer. There is also a southern-hemisphere jet stream, lying for the most part, like its northern counterpart, between the 30th and 55th parallels of latitude.

At any rate, I've found a good specimen of this river in the sky. I've also found, just as the New York weatherman predicted, a massive cloud formation looming to the east of *Charlie*. Even at twenty-nine thousand feet it towers above us, and I keep climbing, skimming through the cloud tops until at thirty-seven thousand feet *Excalibur III* rides smoothly above the elements. The sky above is empty and blue; below, there is a violent winter storm, its upper canopy of white cloud giving it a look of deceitful innocence.

I set course for the next weather ship, *Ocean Station Jig*, six hundred and fifty miles due east of *Charlie*. Out here in the middle of the Atlantic the shorelines of both Newfoundland and Ireland are nearly a thousand miles away. With my new bloom of health I'm beginning to enjoy hitchhiking seven miles high. At least for now, there are no tough decisions to make.

The engine is running smoothly even with the outside

air-temperature reading close to 70 degrees below zero; the cockpit is snug and warm with plenty of heat flowing from the engine, and the sun pours in from over the starboard wing. There is no trace of frost on the cockpit canopy, and except for the altimeter indication of thirty-seven thousand feet, I have no sense of altitude. My undersized cockpit is without pressure, and I have no pressure suit; yet here I sit, in nothing more protective than my unglamorous red flannels, and find nothing much to complain about except that the parachute I'm sitting on isn't getting any softer.

I keep a wary eye on the engine oil indications, as well as the engine coolant temperature. If those little pointers move as much as one-sixteenth of an inch in the wrong direction, there will be nothing but trouble.

The cloudy weather below appears to be lowering, so I descend to thirty-five thousand feet. Breaks appear in the clouds, allowing brief glimpses of the sea. It is a mass of distant whitecaps; the ocean is seething with the wind. Up here above the weather, the air has been perfectly smooth in spite of the swift flow of the jet stream. Since passing Boston several hours ago, we've been on top of all clouds and there hasn't been a ripple in the sky.

All this time, even during that groggy hour, I have been juggling the fuel supply, shifting the fuel tank selector from one wing tank to the other in order to keep the aircraft in lateral trim. I am trying to drain as much fuel out of these tanks as possible without running them dry. If this should happen, the engine would quit, and there would be dead silence until I switched to another tank. Out here over the sea, I don't relish this kind of silence. Therefore, to keep matters serene I maintain a careful watch on the fuel pressure. Shortly before approaching weather ship *Jig,* I shift to the main tank in the wing-center section, which should carry us through to London with plenty to spare. If there should be trouble with the terminal weather, I can reduce speed and continue hundreds of miles beyond London to some refuge on the continent.

With the fuel problem out of the way, I transfer the remainder of the reserve oil supply into the main tank. Now I can take my eye off the oil-pressure gauge and concentrate more on the radio. I am an hour east of *Charlie* and should be close to *Jig*. Because there is no way to perceive drift, I'm not aware we've been blown to the north, off course. Hoping for a position fix I make radio contact with a Scottish gentleman on *Jig* whose burr fairly rattles my earphones. He requests a long transmission so that he can take a bearing on my signal. He also picks the P-51 up in his radar and gives a bearing and distance from his position. Though seventy miles off course, I've no reason to complain. The speed between weather ships has been a brisk five hundred thirty miles an hour.

An east-southeasterly heading soon pins down the west leg of the Shannon radio range. Thirty minutes past *Jig* the signal from the range is loud and clear. The aural tone is unbroken, verifying we're back on course. This is sweet music. The navigation problem suddenly becomes very simple.

Far below, the blue-black Atlantic shows through a layer of broken clouds, and now the surface of the ocean appears dead calm with no trace of whitecap. Before long I catch a glimpse of jagged rocks jutting out of the sea, marking the seaward end of the rugged mountain called Brandon Head on the mainland of Ireland. Never has the land of the shamrock looked more inviting.

The landfall is a few minutes late. The course to London has taken the P-51 out of the jet stream into winds that are light and variable. The free ride is over.

I call the control tower at the Shannon airport to request the London weather and a reclearance over Shannon, Strumble, and Bristol instead of over the St. Eval beacon near Land's End. We cross the Shannon radio range at

1645 GMT, four hours and ten minutes from Gander, Newfoundland, having averaged eight miles a minute for the water crossing.

Ireland is covered by clouds, and the terrain is visible only through occasional breaks. I set course for St. David's Head, the westernmost tip of Wales. The Air Traffic Controller gives reclearance to London as requested, to descend to nineteen thousand five hundred feet over Bristol.

The Shannon control tower suddenly comes on the air with a warning message. "N-one-two-oh-two, visibility at London is fourteen hundred yards in smoke and fog. Better hurry, Charlie." It's the voice of my friend Ned Stapleton.

An hour ago, the visibility was eight miles, and there has been a rapid worsening of the weather. My sixth sense, the one with the built-in "air sense" antenna, vibrates a little, but I give no consideration to returning to Shannon. There is sufficient fuel to experiment with London, and then go elsewhere.

The sun is setting as we cross the Irish Sea. St. David's Head and the mountains of Wales pass swiftly below, almost obscured by the gathering darkness. At 1725 we're over Bristol, flying at nineteen thousand five hundred feet. It is now full night.

Anticipating a fast descent from Bristol to London, I call London Radar for a clearance. There's a note of reassuring hospitality in the Englishman's precise instructions. "Cleared to descend," he tells me. "Cross Woodley at five thousand." Woodley is a radio beacon on the eastern outskirts of the city of Reading and is twenty miles west of the London airport at Heathrow. The London controller advises that airport visibility is still fourteen hundred yards, surface wind calm, altimeter setting 30.03, landing runway 28, to the west.

I fumble around in the dark cockpit trying to fasten the seat belt and shoulder harness, but my movements are so restricted in the crowded little cage it's impossible to make connections. While thus preoccupied, with hands off the controls, the airplane dives steeply to an excessive velocity, slewing uncomfortably in a high-speed skid because the rudder is trimmed for flying at a more reasonable speed. I pull the nose up gently and reduce power to slow down my skidding fighter.

I decide to ignore the seat belt and shoulder harness. We're descending thousands of feet each minute in the black night, and it's more important to fly and navigate precisely. London Radar spots the P-51's tiny blip after passing Bristol. Over Reading he turns control over to the London Approach Radar for a precision-instrument approach to the runway.

There is a glow through the clouds as *Excalibur III*, at full throttle and with the airspeed touching the red line, crosses the lights of Reading on a heading for the Woodley radio beacon. I hear the conversation of airline traffic holding near Epsom, to the south of London.

"Steer ninety-five degrees. There's no speed restriction," the controller advises. "We're holding the airlines at Epsom."

No further instructions are necessary. The 95 degree heading splits the end of the runway. I pull over to the right to adjust the downwind leg for the landing. It's time to slow down. For the first time since leaving New York my faithful Rolls-Royce gets a respite from full throttle.

They are firing flares up into the murky night from the approach end of 28 right, the duty runway. It's a heart-warming display. There's no better airport anywhere, but tonight London Airport looks better than ever. In fact, it looks altogether beautiful in its black envelope of smog.

I line up the approach lights. The flaps are down and so is the landing gear as we sweep low at a hundred and fifty miles an hour.

"Cleared to land" are the final words of welcome in my earphones.

A film of oil on the windshield blurs the visibility from the cockpit, so I feel for the runway in a fast landing. The P-51 is on the London concrete at 1738 London time, seven hours and forty-eight minutes from takeoff at New York, a new record for the Atlantic by an hour and seven minutes.

Even with a tailwind thirty-five miles an hour less than expected, my "flying gas tank," so renamed by the London newsmen, still averaged four hundred and fifty miles an hour for the thirty-five hundred nonstop miles. No piston-engine airplane is likely to fly the Atlantic faster.

But there was another reason to celebrate. This final test flight revealed the true greatness of my airplane. The Arctic was suddenly a lot closer. Only the North Sea now separated *Excalibur III* from its launching strip in Norway.

Two days later I was eastbound again—from New York to London—this time in charge of a Pan American Stratocruiser. A passenger stopped me in the aisle to confide, "Captain, I hear a Pan Am pilot just flew across here on one engine—all by himself—you know, solo. Must be crazy."

"Must be," I said.

CHAPTER NINE

Through the Purple Haze

On May 29, 1951, there wasn't a cloud in the sky the whole length of Norway. Along the route from Oslo to Bardufoss a myriad of mountains thrust their snowy crests into the friendly sunshine.

New York would be seventy-five hundred miles from Oslo by way of the North Pole, and I had no plans for a rest along the route. Therefore I was grateful to find the first leg of the flight so free of difficulty. On a misty day the fighter airstrip in the fjord at Bardufoss might have been hard to find. In good weather it was easy.

I am obliged to the German *Luftwaffe* of World War II for putting Bardufoss on the map. It was the Germans who thoughtfully laid down this concrete strip along the bottom of Bardufoss fjord which could eventually accommodate this one-man polar expedition.

Of course, there was an earlier reason for the existence

of this airstrip. Not many years ago the battleship *Tirpitz* was bottled up by the British in the nearby fjord at Tromsö, and the pride of the German navy needed fighter protection.

But Britain's Royal Air Force managed to sink the *Tirpitz,* anyway, and it has been quiet around Bardufoss ever since. But not today. My P-51 has attracted a great deal of attention since its arrival two hours ago. In less than an hour more, at 1500 Greenwich Mean Time, the little red airplane will be on its way up the 20th east meridian toward the top of the world, and from there to Alaska, and New York.

Five minutes of this final hour have been set aside for privacy and reflection. Eleven hours have passed since I climbed out of bed at Oslo in the early dawn. My flight plan is ten and a half hours across the Arctic to Fairbanks, and nine and a half more to cover the thirty-four hundred mile stretch from Fairbanks to New York. Right now, after chasing down so many details, I feel tired just contemplating the long journey across the Arctic and North America in that tiny cockpit.

The bottom of an upturned bucket in a dimly lit corner of the base headquarters latrine offers a place to sit in solitude and contemplate what lies ahead. Resting my head on my hands, I close my eyes and do some thinking.

From this humble sanctuary the prospect of flying alone across the top of the world is not the same as it was many months ago back home on Long Island. Everything seemed much simpler when I first hatched this ambitious idea. Now some unforeseen details are staring me in the face.

The takeoff will be one of those details. One end of the fighter airstrip at Bardufoss abuts against the western extremity of the fjord, thus dictating takeoffs in one direction only—down the fjord to the east. But what about that westerly tailwind on the runway? At last reading it was seven knots. Just a few more knots and the one mile of pavement won't be quite enough.

And what about those celestial precomputations? The final corrections were made in Oslo several days ago. From now on, it's blind faith in the numbers against the readings on my timepieces, my three watches. If a crucial digit is incorrect, there's no telling where my landfall will be. Speaking of landfalls, the forecast for Point Barrow indicates the north coast of Alaska will have bad weather. It might be better to rest and go tomorrow.

Tomorrow! Good grief, man! Something worse will crop up! I jump angrily from the bucket, jostling it among a cluster of brooms and mops which clatter to the floor. The self-chastisement gets me going again. I must get on to the briefing.

A group of Norwegian officers is waiting in the briefing room. Captain Helge Anonsen is a stocky, red-haired officer with a big spread of bushy mustache. He shows a chart of the Spitzbergen area, designated in Norwegian as Svalbard. Captain Anonsen is an expert on Arctic survival. He explains in perfect English and says, "You will find good emergency landings at these points." He carefully outlines each area with light pencil marks and then goes into detail. There is some question about the Svalbard weather. A cold front is moving in from the west.

The situation would have to be really grim to cause a landing on Spitzbergen. Nevertheless it's a good idea to store the information. In case of trouble, that frostbitten land could suddenly look like an island paradise. Captain Anonsen continues to give out a store of pertinent detail. Of special importance, he reveals that the radio beacons on Bear Island and Spitzbergen will be operating continuously until my airplane has passed the point of no return. He has also arranged for rescue support during the flight's early stage. "We have a Catalina flying boat patrolling between Bear Island and Spitzbergen. It departed Tromsö three hours ago and is equipped to help you if you're forced down between Bear Island and eighty degrees north. The northern limit of its patrol will be the north coast of Spitzbergen. Their radio will stand by on one two one point five for your progress reports. The Catalina's call sign will be 'Blackbird.' Yours will be 'Snow White.' "

I feel a warm sense of gratitude toward these rugged descendants of the Vikings. They've gone out of their way to help an American stranger, and that goes for every Norwegian who has had any connection with helping to get this trip underway, from General Odd Bull of the Norwegian Royal Air Force on down. Captain Anonsen reveals a squadron secret. "You know, Captain, we've been trying to get permission to fly our own Catalina to the pole and back. If your flight is successful, it will help get us that permission."

"I'll express my appreciation by reaching Alaska," I assure him with fingers crossed, and reassure myself by just saying it.

A final time check confirms the setting of my three wrist watches. Accurate time is of special importance when flying the Arctic, not only for using the sextant but for steering as well.

The communications officer comes in search of the flight plan. We go outside to scribble it off, using the fender of a truck as a desk. The numbers roll easily out of the back of my head where they've been circulating for weeks. Within two minutes the flight plan has been formally inscribed and is ready for radio transmission to Alaska.

In the midst of this process, Lieutenant Colonel Jon Tvedte, the fighter commander at Bardufoss, returns from the refueling area to escort me to the airplane. He brings good news. The starboard aft section of the cockpit canopy which tore loose and fell from the aircraft while circling Bardufoss for the landing has been located by a search party

Transatlantic circles over the American-Export liner *Excalibur*—sunk during World War II

The first flying *Excalibur* which set a record for the first non-stop airline flight across the Atlantic with passengers and mail

Excalibur III, my private fighter, which set a transatlantic speed record that still stands

Departing from Oslo for Bardufoss, Fairbanks and New York—7,500 miles away

Excalibur III landing at Bardufoss before attempting the first solo flight across the Arctic Ocean

Loaded down with 865 gallons of fuel, the tail-heavy *Excalibur III* roars down the runway

Excalibur III returns to Idlewild Airport after its solo flight over the North Pole

With ground-crew chief of my B-47 bomber at Lake Charles
Air Force Base, preparing for star-tracking tests

Excalibur IV, a Republic F84-F Thunderstreak fighter stripped of its guns and loaded with electronic equipment. Its star tracker is visible on top of the nose

Operation Sharkbait. With my wingmen, Captain Martinez (left) and Major Tomlinson (right), before take-off

Flying the lead aircraft of Operation Julius Caesar, I take off from Wethersfield RAF Station for Eielson Air Force Base, Alaska

Operation completed. Taxiing *Excalibur V*, my North American F100-F Supersabre, to the flight line at Eielson Air Force Base

in the fjord. It's astonishing that anyone could find such an odd piece of canopy in the wide expanse of drifted snow. It's even more impressive to meet men sufficiently vigorous and frugal to go looking for such a needle in a haystack. I had expected they would merely rivet a metal plate over the missing section. Now *Excalibur III* will look as sleek and shiny as ever.

Jon Tvedte runs an excellent outfit, judged by the way things are done at his fighter outpost on the north fringe of Europe. Like many of the men in the Norwegian RAF, he speaks English with hardly an accent. At lunch an hour ago he framed a now-familiar question.

"Captain, what's the *real* reason for this journey?" he inquired, with a sympathetic gleam in the eye. "I expected to see some advertisements inscribed on the side of your aircraft."

"It's noncommercial," I assured him as a starter.

I have no pat answer for this question about motivation. It always depends on who asks. Because Colonel Tvedte's philosophy appeared to be not much different from my own, the answer came more easily. Not only that—most Norwegians have a special rapport with the far north, which makes this kind of expedition especially interesting to them. Some people can ask me this same question and draw a blank, especially if they're digging for a confession of insanity.

But to Tvedte the explanation is simple. I explain that twenty years of military and airline flying, plus test-hopping fighters, plus running a tramp airline on the side, along with a capacity for quick and easy celestial navigation, all add up to what's needed for an odd job such as this.

I don't mention the "experts" who warned me against flying the Arctic. If they are right, and I am wrong, or vice versa, the matter will be resolved within the next ten hours.

"Looks like it's tailor-made," concedes the Norwegian.

We move on to the flight line where the conversation

changes to technical details. *Excalibur III*, since arrival from Oslo, has stood poised in takeoff position on the end of the runway.

The P-51 looks trim and ready, although its heavy fuel load is revealed by a thin trickle of gasoline flowing along the undersurface of the right wing. This is a chronic problem, stemming from the lack of fuel cells in the wing, which is full of gasoline from tip to tip. The outer skin of the wing has been plugged here and there with zinc chromate paste to stop fuel leaks which have been much worse on other occasions. So I'm pleased it's now only a trickle. The total fuel load—eight hundred and sixty-five gallons, all carried internally—is enough to fly from here to Fairbanks and almost a thousand miles beyond.

Because there is more than a half-ton weight of fuel in the fuselage tank behind the pilot's seat, the airplane rests heavily on its tail wheel. This is the Achilles heel of the expedition, and explains why a spare tire has been nestled on my shoulder, further shrinking the crowded cockpit all the way from Oslo. It will now be left behind.

Lieutenant Gaarde emerges from under the airplane's tail, detaching himself from a cluster of Norwegian Air Force mechanics who have been swarming over *Excalibur III* since its arrival. The lieutenant, who is engineering officer of Bardufoss' Vampire jet squadron, understands every rivet on the airplane. He has worked with P-51s before, which is my good fortune. Now he is especially concerned with the tail-wheel strut. Because of corrosion he has found it impossible to pump up the strut sufficiently to support the fuel weight properly. A good lurch would break the tire.

Nothing can be done about this problem except to inspect the runway for rough spots with the idea of steering the smoothest possible takeoff course. A trip down the runway in a jeep turns out to be useful in other ways as well, affording the opportunity to make a mental note of various runway landmarks for gauging takeoff performance. There are other last-minute preparations: checking the sextant, stowing the navigation gear and inspecting the stowage of survival equipment contributed by the United States Air Force. Included is a .45 caliber pistol. I hope I don't need it.

My apparel for the Arctic is less conservative than last winter's selection for the North Atlantic speed record to London. However, the sport jacket, slacks, white shirt, and red-striped necktie are covered by the same good-luck threadbare summer flying suit. A hunting jacket and flying boots have been added, but I've dispensed with the long red underwear and the useless life vest. If forced down, I'll be the most snappily dressed tourist ever to roam the Arctic ice pack.

The work is finished and the men step away, leaving *Excalibur III* standing alone. For a moment I'm lost in admiration. It's a beautiful airplane. Its deep-maroon lacquer is freshly polished and glistening in the afternoon sun. A small American flag is emblazoned on the side of the fuselage below the cockpit. Stenciled behind the cockpit is the word "experimental" which reminds me this is no ordinary flying machine. In the center of the fuselage is a black hawk in a white circle, my own good-luck emblem.

I climb aboard and Lieutenant Gaarde battens down the canopy after stuffing me into the cockpit. The added array of navigation and survival gear makes it smaller than ever. This will be my prison for ten and a half hours.

I am wedged in with both upper arms jammed against the canopy tracks, and can barely turn to right or left, although my forearms and hands are free. If anything falls to the cockpit floor I could not retrieve it—an extra hazard that calls for further precautions. Then, too, there's always the possibility of a leg cramp, but I'll meet that problem when and if it comes.

At the flick of a switch the Rolls-Royce Merlin comes

alive, then settles to an even staccato for a minute of warm-up. All the gauges read as they should. I clamp on my oxygen mask.

Lieutenant Gaarde raises his hand and points at his wrist watch. My hand goes to the throttle.

At 1458—two minutes early—the chocks are away. I'll squander those extra minutes in the fjord on the climbout.

I release the brakes. The little red airplane starts gathering momentum, riding heavily on its delicate tail wheel. The elevator airload gradually eases its contact with the rough pavement. Halfway down the runway the takeoff is committed. There can be no stopping this fuel-heavy vehicle now. One problem disappeared when the tail wheel came free of the ground, but the troublesome tailwind is adding critical footage to the takeoff. The tail-heaviness, due to the fuselage tank fuel, causes the airplane to be so unstable that extra speed is needed for it to become safely airborne. Because the runway is barely a mile long I must keep the main wheels on the ground until the last few yards of pavement.

The end of the runway is coming up with a rush. A dip near the end is followed by a rise. The airspeed meter tells me the airplane will fly. I pull back on the stick. *Excalibur III* is launched as if by a catapult, then staggers along a few feet above the floor of the fjord, struggling to gain a few extra knots of speed. Not far from the end of the runway a knoll rises in front of me. There is no chance to ease above it, so I ease around it, slightly to the right. Suddenly the ground drops away in a gentle downslope and now it's clear sailing down the fjord. The valley widens and stretches in an easterly direction with towering, snow-covered mountains on both sides.

The 20th east meridian, which is my track to the pole, lies several minutes ahead. At 1506 on the Greenwich clock I'll slip over the rim of the mountains and turn north. But right now there are a few moments to look around. The airplane wallows clumsily, but the higher speed and altitude make the instability problem only a minor inconvenience. On the left side a pair of Vampire jets are coming up from astern—my Norwegian friends seeing me off. The weather is cloudless, with the sparkling, clear air affording a scene of desolate grandeur as the P-51 climbs above the mountains. Over the nose, stretching all the way from Tromsö to North Cape, is a spectacular panorama of the Arctic coast of Norway, studded with precipitous snow-clad mountains interlaced by the blue-black waters of numerous valleys and fjords.

Excalibur III intersects the 20th meridian, its highway to the Pole, and heads due north. My friends in the jets dip their wings in a goodbye salute, then peel off and turn back toward Bardufoss. They're the last men I'll see until I reach Alaska.

The coast of Norway recedes, and soon a cloud layer intervenes to blot out the ocean. I'm flying into a void, and will soon lose all touch with the world I know. Only one tie remains. Off the left wing hangs a glistening ball—the sun.

The P-51 continues to wallow, although it flies better as the tail-heavy fuel behind my seat is gradually used up. Soon, with the center of gravity moved forward again, it will stop galloping and start flying like a real airplane.

After leveling off at fifteen thousand feet I discover I'm too finicky about holding a precise altitude, as if the sky were dense with traffic. But there's no air traffic up here unless some Russian has strayed from his base in Franz Josef Land, or an American B-29 is out reconnoitering the weather from Alaska. Otherwise the Arctic is my private ocean.

Although nothing stands in the way of my frisking between altitudes in uninhibited fashion, the need for accurate navigation suggests I stick with the stodgy flight plan. This calls for climbing to twenty-two thousand feet after passing Spitzbergen, then up to twenty-five thousand one hour after passing the Pole. Right now it's best to hold fifteen thousand. Until north of Spitzbergen a strong north-westerly quartering headwind is forecast for the higher levels. Because there is no cockpit pressurization I'll not climb higher than twenty-five thousand feet at any time, unless more altitude is needed to keep the sun in sight. I have unpleasant memories of the oxygen difficulty which almost put me to sleep and out of business during January's speed run to London.

I'm beginning to suspect my ten-dollar magnetic compass. Still, it has done a good job at more civilized latitudes, and has long since paid its way. Now I'll drag out the more expensive one. This one—the sun compass—cost $12.50, war surplus.

Accommodating the sun compass involves setting up a metal bar across the cockpit in front of my seat. After squirming around in my cage the compass is installed on a mount that travels to right or left the bar to which-ever side of the cockpit is required for sighting. I slide the gadget to the left end of the bar, and it's ready to go. The sun is over the left wing, slightly aft, and some 20 degrees above the horizon.

When the minute hand of the clock shows 1530 GMT my bearing on the sun should read 255 degrees, or 15 de-grees behind the left wing. After setting up the correct numbers on the sun compass, I gently turn the airplane until the shadow of the sun falls between a pair of lubber lines on the sighting bar. That's exactly the course I must steer. There will be no error in this device if I did my homework right.

Steering by the sun is not a difficult task. In fact, taking into account the estimated ground speed, it's necessary only to steer gradually left toward the sun, lessening the angle between the aircraft nose and the sun by 2 degrees at the end of each ten-minute interval. Eventually, some two hours after passing the North Pole, the sun will have come around over the nose. By that time the angular change every ten minutes will have increased to three degrees, and thereafter I'll gradually steer away from my celestial guidepost. At Point Barrow, the sun should be well to the right of the P-51's nose.

Operating the sun compass is so absorbing I almost forget where I am.

We approach Bear Island, which is a Norwegian pinpoint near the 20th meridian. As it passes abeam, the radio direction finder makes a leisurely swing to the left. By timing the swing, I fix the position some twenty miles to the east, which is directly astride the chosen flight path. The airplane is tracking due north, angling a few degrees to the left to correct for the drift of the northwesterly wind. There will be one more radio check when abeam the Svalbard radio station on West Spitzbergen. After that the radio will be shut down.

Spitzbergen, for the past half century, has been a dramatic name in the history of the Arctic, and a jumping-off place for many an expedition into the far north. I'd like to get a look at this rugged Norwegian island, but today at fifteen thousand feet it's not to be. The cloud deck is unbroken. I content myself with the impersonal swing of the radio direction finder.

I'm due on the air with a position report for the Norwegian flying boat. This air-sea-rescue Catalina, commanded by Lieutenant Johansen, should now be patrolling between Bear Island and Spitzbergen.

"Blackbird from Snow White."

My first call brings a faint reply. We're still some distance from one another, and my receiver barely picks up Blackbird's signal. After acknowledging the position report, the voice asks how I'm doing. The Catalina is flying below the overcast in the vicinity of Spitzbergen. It's encouraging to talk with someone, especially the friendly Johansen, who treats this alien polar expedition as if it were flying his own flag of Norway.

The Spitzbergen radio beacon passes abeam at 1716. I give the Norwegian Catalina a final position report.

"Blackbird from Snow White. Over Spitzbergen beacon at 1716."

"Goodbye and good luck." That's the last voice I'll hear until I reach Alaska.

"So long, Blackbird. Many thanks." I shut down all radio.

Excalibur III, and the sun, are now my only companions.

Soon afterward we cross 80 degrees north. The upper winds should be tapering off. We climb to twenty-two thousand. The climb at high engine revolutions helps to clean up the sensitive spark plugs. Settling down to cruise at that level, the engine purrs without a discordant murmur. This engine has only one minor quirk, the possibility of accumulating lead deposits on the spark plugs while cruising at low engine revolutions. The cure is to increase power for a few moments every now and then to burn out the offending deposits.

Another engine characteristic deserves special care. This type is liquid-cooled. I must be wary of any malfunction, especially the position of the coolant shutter, that would cause the coolant to overheat and boil away. Therefore the coolant gauge comes in for its fair share of attention.

But this is a rugged engine, and if I manage it properly there'll be little to worry about. On the speed run from New York to London, it was ramrodded at maximum allowable power during the entire trip and thrived on it.

The P-51 flies like a real airplane again, now that the tail-heaviness is gone. The fuel from the rear tank has been used up, so I switch to one of the wing tanks. Because it feeds from only one side at a time, the airplane gradually grows wing-heavy. Therefore I shift the fuel source from one wing to another at half-hour intervals to keep lateral balance. Such details—the continuous routine of adjusting the sun compass, shifting from one fuel tank to another, keeping an eye on all the gauges, occasionally running the engine to high revolutions, operating the sextant and performing other navigational details—keep me so busy there's no time for thinking about trouble. Even the loneliness of the Arctic hasn't registered—yet.

The sun is slightly forward of the wing now. I preset the sextant according to the precomputations and squint through the sextant sunshade. The sun is thus reduced to a tiny green pea. It wobbles around a little, but its average position is right in the middle of the sextant's bubble horizon. That means I'm still on the 20th meridian, on the desired track. At 83 degrees north latitude the clouds suddenly break away, revealing a limitless ocean of unbroken ice reaching out beyond the distant horizon.

To a traveler in the company of others this might be just another magnificent view. But to me, alone in the Arctic, the panorama verges on the supernatural. A thin purple haze softens the stark whiteness of the snow-covered ice, casting a tinted glow on the rippled surface of the icecap. Little puffs of cloud hang motionless.

A man on the surface of the ice would find those ripples to be more than formidable. A forced landing would be a rough affair.

I wonder how many unfulfilled polar expeditions lie frozen beneath the innocent white face of this provocative ocean.

Which brings to mind a conversation with General Riiser-Larsen several days ago in Oslo. More than a quarter of a century ago, he was Amundsen's pilot on an unsuccessful quest for the Pole by air. Having lived on the surface for many months after being forced down, he wasn't optimistic about a forced landing in a P-51. Because of conflicting ocean currents the ice on the European side of the Pole is generally tumbled and rough. It will be much less corrugated on the Alaskan side.

Right now the engine is running without a trace of roughness, but if it should fail, there would be no choice but to ride the airplane down to whatever kind of landing the surface might afford. It would be futile to bail out and leave behind the survival gear which could not be attached to my parachute. "If you're forced down north of latitude eighty-five, you'll find no living thing," warned Riiser-Larsen, recollecting his own experience.

I banish such thoughts, and go back to my sun compass.

The airplane drones on past 85 degrees north. The white spinner on the nose points directly up the meridian. The haze is deepening, causing a further reddening of the sun which further highlights the spectacular glow of the icecap. My little red fighter sweeps on past 86—87—88—89 degrees north latitude. The sun-shaded green pea wobbles in the middle of the bubble whenever the sextant is pointed at the sun. There's almost no wind now, and no correction for drift. The sun is closer to the nose. It is low in the northwest, hanging like a red ball in the sky, some 21 degrees above the horizon. The haze to the north has continued to thicken, reducing the visibility to a few miles. I search the northeast sky for the moon. It should be popping up over the horizon. But the moon fails to show. My eyes strain through the purple haze in vain. Could there be a defect in my celestial computations? Where or when could I have made a mistake? Am I flying in circles?

Steady, fellow. That haze *must* be blotting out the daylight moon.

The sextant is preset for the sun's declination. At 1955, according to my reckoning, *Excalibur III* should be crossing the top of the world.

At 1955, GMT I point the sextant at the sun. The little green pea of the sun wobbles once again in the center of the bubble. Suddenly I'm heading due south.

The sensation of reaching a long-sought goal was fleeting—over before I realized it had happened. I was robbed of the chance to savor it.

Now every direction is south. It's like sitting on top of a giant maypole, faced with a pick of countless streamers, one of which leads to Point Barrow. Others lead to Siberia, to Greenland, or back to Norway. The choice has long since been made. It means holding the sun steady off to the left of the airplane's nose, exactly where it was during the last few minutes before reaching the Pole. This selects the right streamer.

But the perspective has changed. A moment ago it was an evening sun in the northwest sky. Now it's a morning sun in the southeast. The airplane didn't flip, nor did the sun. It simply gained twelve hours on the clock. We should be arriving in Fairbanks, Alaska, before we left Norway. This oddity will be of interest to stamp collectors who pay close attention to dates and times of stamp cancellations. My mail-sack contains three thousand covers of transpolar mail addressed to the Damon Runyon Cancer Fund in New York. These are scheduled to be canceled at a time and date preceding the departure from Norway.

There's one other piece of mail aboard—a letter to Santa Claus from a small boy, my son Chris. Opening the sliding window a crack, I watch the airstream whip it away. Following it is a book of matches inscribed by friends from the Savoy Hotel in London. Maybe the ghost of Robert E. Peary could use a match.

The airplane bores on along the 160th west meridian. As the sky condition changes, the haze is transformed into ice crystals. These shimmering frost particles fail to blot out the sun, but horizontal visibility is reduced to nothing. Looking straight down it's still possible to glimpse the ice, but I go on instruments.

The little ten-dollar magnetic compass reads an unsteady 60 degrees which amounts to 120 degrees of error, but the $12.50 model is doing very well. In spite of the ice-fog, the sun is still casting its guiding shadow down the sight bar. The glistening bull's-eye in the sky is now moving around the horizon at 15 degrees an hour and will soon be speeding up to 18. Two hours from now the sun is scheduled to be directly over the nose. Then it will be high noon on the 160th meridian of west longitude.

At 85 degrees north latitude on the southward leg, the flight plan dictates a climb to twenty-five thousand feet. I pay close heed to the oxygen equipment as the aircraft levels off at the higher level, which is still well below the top of the crystalline haze. The oxygen mask has been only a minor discomfort, although it fits so tightly it creases the face. A check of the oxygen supply shows it exceeds the fuel endurance, and there's no shortage of fuel. A flick of the switch transfers the reserve oil supply to the engine tank. Fuel, oxygen, oil. Everything checks.

The monotony of being suspended in the white firmament of ice-fog surrounded by the vast emptiness of frozen ocean allows the mind to wander. Even the name of the airplane becomes a matter for consideration. The name has been changed since its last visit to Fairbanks. On that preparatory visit last August the name of this little ship was *Stormy Petrel*. Today the engine cowling displays *Excalibur III*. On the radio the airplane is called N-1202, a number which decorates the wings and tail.

I've never been too superstitious before, but there may be something in a name. A stormy petrel is a small, long-range bird of the sea. It is also reputed to be a herald of ill fortune. Misfortune dogged this airplane while it bore the name. Every flight I made from its original base at Burbank in California produced some mechanical problem that taxed my ingenuity. Some of the difficulties were circumvented by devising odd procedures; others just cost a lot of money, which I was running out of. The new equipment needed more extensive test-flying than had been planned, and this couldn't be left safely undone. Being the lone backer of this project, the bills and the bad luck were on my back. When I started suspecting the name of my airplane, it became time for a change.

Excalibur III has done better. My other *Excaliburs* were lucky ships when I flew them, and I haven't forgotten the story of King Arthur. There was magic in his sword *Excalibur*. There is magic in this little airplane.

I'm still flying on instruments in a white bowl. The sun has come around directly over the nose, a perfect setup for a check of our southward progress. The sextant shows our position to be astride the 80th parallel of north latitude within a minute of flight plan. This is the first positive check of groundspeed since passing Spitzbergen. I'm holding closer to flight plan than I had dared anticipate.

The cockpit heater has been shut down, but I'm perspiring in the glare of the noonday sun and from the uncontrollable excess of heat pouring back from the engine. I was later to find out I had lost ten pounds between Oslo and New York. The outside air temperature is a chilly minus 40. It must be plus 80 or even warmer inside.

But the dehydration at least solves one problem. I won't need to disturb that milk bottle stowed under my seat. Although a pee-tube is standard plumbing on a modern fighter, my P-51 is not elegant enough for such sophisticated apparatus.

I contemplate the ham sandwich in the brown paper sack stowed up forward against the windshield. But it doesn't stir the appetite. Besides, it would be too much trouble manipulating the oxygen mask.

My thoughts are now riveted on Alaska. The coastline is less than six hundred miles away.

Some recollections of Fairbanks come to mind. I wondered idly about the weather and the reception we'll get. My feelings about Fairbanks are colored by memories of the visit there last August. It wasn't a hearty welcome when I flew north from Los Angeles to reconnoiter the area, and to become familiar with problems which might occur when approaching this Alaskan metropolis from the north.

Ladd Field, the port of entry at Fairbanks, is a military airport with a split personality. It houses some of the civilian airlines, too. To fly into Ladd, considering the war going on in the Far East, an itinerant pilot must first seek permission via the Pentagon in Washington. Having received this, he notifies Fairbanks by way of normal CAA communications from his last port of call. This message warns of the estimated time of arrival, and also gives routine statistics about the airplane and pilot. All this was duly accomplished, and *Excalibur III* arrived over Fairbanks precisely as planned. Fortunately, a heavy thunderstorm saturated the area at that particular time. The inhospitable weather turned out to be a protective cloak against a more drastic problem. My departure message had misfired somewhere in the chain of communications.

If the P-51 had been a civilian-type airplane, the mistake would have been of minor consequence. But the Korean War was at the height of its fury and everyone was remembering Pearl Harbor, for good and valid reasons. Now here on another Sunday came an unannounced fighter, deep maroon in color and oddly adorned. The gunners were eager for target practice. The cloudburst cheated them.

After I taxied to the ramp, a young Air Force lieutenant, drenched by the rain, came out to investigate the unannounced invader. Base Operations had received no message relating to such an aircraft. However, after I flashed a few documents, the lad thawed out and offered congratulations.

"Congratulations for what?" I inquired.

"For not getting shot down," he retorted with a grin.

. . .

Today in Fairbanks there should be no such problem. Pan American Airways, which is supervising my public relations, specializes in worldwide communications. A half-dozen messages sent ahead to Fairbanks will precede my arrival.

I feel a trickle of warm moisture flowing onto my upper lip. Holding my breath in the thin air I remove the oxygen mask to find it smeared with blood.

On the ground a nosebleed isn't much of a problem. But in the air you wonder if it will ever stop. In a crowded little cage at twenty-five thousand above the Arctic ice with no cabin pressure, it takes an effort to be optimistic.

I must stanch the flow of blood, and still inhale enough oxygen from the mask to keep my lungs in a healthy state. I manipulate the control stick with my knees and apply a handkerchief between quick whiffs from the oxygen mask.

I'm fastidious about the flight plan, and reject the idea of diving to a lower altitude where it would be safe to breathe without oxygen. Besides disturbing my fuel reckoning, it would be impossible to steer precisely down there. I would lose sight of the sun in the clouds and ice-fog.

After a few minutes the flow stops. Apparently the long exposure to oxygen, together with the excessive heat flowing into the cockpit from the engine, had dried up and damaged the interior of my nostrils. Fortunately the blood has now clotted.

I strap the mask back on with the hope this messy problem won't reoccur. It threatens to ruin the décor of my cockpit.

I start tinkering with the radio compass which has been shut down since Spitzbergen. While it's warming up I crank in the frequency of Point Barrow radio and turn up the volume, not expecting to hear much of anything. But suddenly there's a crash of background static. The radio comes to life. From out of the noise comes an unmistakable signal in Morse code—PBA—PBA—PBA—the identification for Point Barrow.

That wonderful cockeyed world is calling us back!

The radio direction finder needle quivers, swings, then comes to rest. Point Barrow is over the nose!

I contemplate the inanimate little sun compass with affectionate esteem. The $12.50 investment has put on a priceless performance across more than two thousand miles of trackless ice. The sextant, too, had a hand in the job, but not nearly as much as this precise little steering device.

At the 75th parallel I put aside my celestial tools, and take leave of the 160th meridian, which has been our track since leaving the Pole. I turn the airplane a few degrees left to pick up a direct heading for Point Barrow. This northernmost outpost of Alaska is now less than three hundred miles away.

The odds against failure have risen sharply, and keep rising as the miles of unbroken ice roll by underneath. Most of the responsibility now rests with the engine, and the thundering Rolls-Royce has never spoken with more authority.

The prospect of seeing land breaks the spell of being out of touch and completely remote from human contact. Moreover, the landfall should occur at the exact place and time spelled out in my flight plan before we left Norway. When *Excalibur III* crosses the coastline of Alaska the Arctic won't be the same ocean it was ten hours ago. It will no longer seem so much of a barrier.

The ice-fog thins enough to allow a few miles' visibility along the frozen ocean. An occasional fissure reveals a glimpse of blue-black water in an expanse of white. Because there is no perceptible horizon, the ice appears to merge indistinctly with the sky. A hundred miles out from Alaska the clouds break off sharply as if sliced with a giant cleaver. To the south is a cloudless sky with visibility to the brink of the earth's curvature. This break in the weather is a surprise bonanza. The forecast this morning held a different prospect.

A vague outline of rising terrain looms at a great distance. Could that be a mountain range or is it a mirage? Perception of land is often tricky at the end of an ocean flight. The shadow of a cloud on the sea can be mistaken for an island. A formation of clouds can look like a mountain range. But the mountains ahead are authentic. I can make out foothills along the lower slopes of lofty mountains. The terrain falls away to the north and then levels out as it approaches what appears to be a coastline. About halfway across the ocean to this snowless area is a large break in the ice. If the snowless terrain is actually the coastline, it appears we're running late, which is perplexing. The last sextant reading showed us within a minute of flight plan. That particular document, so hastily scribbled on the truck fender at Bardufoss, calls for passing over Point Barrow at 2348 on the Greenwich clock.

At 2347 the radio compass needle swings all the way around and points astern. *Excalibur III* is one minute ahead of schedule. A steep turn allows a visual inspection which validates the radio compass. Directly below on the edge of the tundra is the pattern of buildings which makes up Point Barrow. The sextant is vindicated. It has been proved utterly honest. The large break in the ice, first seen a few minutes ago, turns out to be at the boundary between ocean and coastline. The vast expanse of tundra, snow-covered and appearing from twenty-five thousand feet as a continuation of the ocean ice, is as flat and bleak as the Arctic itself.

Arrival over the Alaskan coastline calls for warming up the radio telephone. But repeated calls to Point Barrow bring no reply. Either my transmitter is out of order on that particular frequency, or Point Barrow isn't receiving for some reason. An assessment of the difficulty isn't possible. At any rate, there is no reasonable option other than to press on toward Fairbanks, and eventually call Ladd Field when sufficiently close.

The flight plan calls for increasing to maximum engine power for the final five hundred miles into Fairbanks, but it is better to loaf along at the transpolar pace of 325 mph and not flog the engine. This will cause the arrival to be a few minutes late, but the local air defense at Fairbanks has had more than ample notice this time. Even the original forecast for the flight, sent ahead more than a month ago, has been followed to the day and hour. The reception should be altogether different from that of last summer's unheralded arrival from Los Angeles.

That first distant glimpse of North America from the Arctic almost an hour ago was the Brooks Range, a mountain barrier astride the route from Point Barrow to Fairbanks. Today the mountains separate winter from spring as *Excalibur III* crosses over at nine thousand feet near the crest of Mt. Alapah. North of the Brooks Range there was nothing but ice-covered tundra. South of the mountains the ridges and hills show no trace of snow. It has become a gentle, summery day with a light haze and an occasional puff of cumulus cloud.

After ten hours behind an oxygen mask it feels good to get the mask off my face and inhale the real atmosphere. I gingerly check the condition of my troublesome nose, and take a look in the rear-vision mirror to make sure all the evidence of the nosebleed has been done away with. I'd rather not confront the public looking so dramatically gruesome.

Dropping lower I fly a few hundred feet above the terrain, becoming aware again of the speed of my airplane, and of the more intimate details of the earth's surface. The occasional farmhouse and village close at hand are heartwarming to behold. Small happenings, too often taken for granted, are a delight to eyes that have been starving on a diet of Arctic ice.

The hours in the far north have invigorated and sharpened my senses. Everything looks better, feels better, and sounds better after you've pushed your luck and won.

I never noticed the two F-80 single-seaters trailing along behind. Years later I discovered they had followed the strange-looking P-51 throughout the last miles to Fairbanks, with guns armed and ready.

The long runway at Ladd Field glistens in the afternoon sun, beckoning to land. I'm eager to straighten out my pretzel-shaped legs before undertaking the thirty-four-hundred-mile nonstop flight to New York, nine and a half more hours of sitting on this rock-hard parachute. New York is home, and the end of a twelve-thousand-mile circuit which began on that frigid night in January when the big wind of the westerlies was swishing high above the Atlantic.

The wheels touch down at Fairbanks ten hours and twenty-seven minutes after leaving the runway at Bardufoss. I pause on a midfield taxi strip and wait for a pair of jet fighters to go screeching by.

This was a heady moment in an hour of triumph. But it was a fleeting moment. The *action* that leads to victory—when the result is still in suspense—leaves the more indelible recollections.

Those hours pushing northward on the other side of the Arctic—when I wasn't totally sure where that glistening red ball in the sky was really taking me—stand out in sharpest relief. The ultimate outcome of the journey appeared to hinge mostly on the accuracy of my mathematics, yet I was vaguely aware of a stronger guiding force than mere numbers.

I was so far removed from the world of reality that the noisy labor of the machinery propelling me was hardly noticed. Alone in the cockpit of my high-flying airplane I became as free as a man can ever be, possessed only by the majestic sweep of the polar icecap, reaching through the purple haze for the top of the world.

PART II

The Supernukes

This book, up to now, has been an aviation story. Part Two contains some other ingredients.

I was not aware of what it was leading me to when I chased that red ball in the sky across the Arctic in my P-51. I knew nothing at that time about the technology of putting a nuclear weapon on its target.

The years that followed the Arctic adventure have been enlightening in this respect, not to mention discomforting; I became a nuclear-delivery "thinker" whose specialty for many years was to help contrive suitable techniques for delivering the smaller thermonuclear weapons.

It has not been easy to "switch off" this thinking process. Therefore I have posed a problem and some questions in a postscript which do not make carefree reading.

Although there are workable solutions, they have no place in this story.

But, the reader may agree, there is quite a problem.

CHAPTER TEN

Think Factory

The best of all rewards for winning in the Arctic was a flying assignment with Colonel Dave Schilling's 31st Strategic Fighter Wing. In the spring of 1952 the fighter escort role of Schilling's three F-84 squadrons was being phased out because someone had learned how to shrink a nuclear weapon into a small package. Henceforth swarms of swift and agile strike fighters, each able to carry megatons of thermonuclear bombs, would take over a significant role in our nation's growing deterrent force.

Schilling, one of America's great fighter aces of the war in Europe, was spearheading this new concept, and he invited me to join the effort. My Arctic voyage in the P-51 had accidentally fitted into the new scheme of things, having proved that a single-seater fighter could traverse the navigationally troublesome Arctic with precision. Therefore such a lightly manned aircraft could also go to work on difficult military targets at long range.

After setting up residence at Turner Air Base in Georgia, home grounds of the 31st Wing of SAC fighters, I underwent combat crew training in the F84-G Thunderjet and became the only civilian fighter pilot in the regular Air Force. Carrying the title "special consultant," my official attachment was to the Fighter Branch of the Directorate of Operations at Air Force Headquarters in the Pentagon. From that key location I was assigned during the early years to the Strategic Air Command, and later to the Tactical Air Command. On three weekends each month I changed hats and went back to my Pan Am Stratocruiser.

My passport around the Air Force circuit was a letter over the signature of a highly placed Pentagon colleague. It simply instructed the clearing authorities at all Air Force bases everywhere to clear my speedy little F-84 wherever and whenever I wanted to go, regardless of weather, and without a shred of red tape.

It was stimulating to become involved in a high-priority government exercise where red tape could be sliced as if it were ordinary bologna. Such cavalier disregard for bureaucratic procedure was astonishing to a former naval aviator with memories of a navy which was too often strait-jacketed by crippling regulations. It seemed too good to last, yet somehow it endured for more than a decade, though with gradually decreasing momentum.

The war in Korea further contributed to loosening things up, as did the absence of a "trade school" tradition in the youngest of our military services. An officer corps which originated mostly on college campuses tended to keep regulations more flexible, and therefore more adaptable to changing requirements.

Schilling, who was superficially casual, though inwardly a pinwheel of animated energy, ignited the fighter nuclear-weapons concept. His congenial swashbuckling, which could be described as an engaging mixture of flamboyance and humility, disarmed the disbelievers, and opened the road toward turning small fighter airplanes into potent nuclear-delivery vehicles.

Breakthroughs in new weapons-delivery systems do not come easily, especially when the spearhead is a mere colonel, no matter how distinguished he may be. Even generals and admirals with almost unlimited authority, who have nursed vital military concepts through to final success, would testify that the road they took was a rough one.

We were starting this project from scratch. There was nothing in the way of proven airborne hardware that could guide our shrunken superweapons precisely to the target. Therefore we organized a small "think factory" at Wing Headquarters which was flippantly referred to as the Schilling Research and Development Center, or SRDC for short.

With me in this "factory" were three young, technically inclined first lieutenants, Lou Setter, Bill Brandt, and Marv Borgensen, who made up in energetic brainpower what they lacked in rank. Schilling, himself, besides being an extraordinarily effective commander, was also a dedicated gadgeteer who spent most of his spare time helping me search the industry for equipment which would take his fighter-bombers precisely where he wanted them to go.

The SRDC, being outside the formal, channelized research and development maze which normally funneled its gadgetry into a bureaucratic thicket known as the WADC (Wright Air Development Center), was less than popular in research and development circles. We pushed hard to expedite development of equipment which would meet the special demands of our new weapons-delivery concept, and in doing so we accidentally trespassed on sacred territory.

Nor could we be totally ignored. SRDC, after all, was a tiny fragment of SAC where the stern visage of the cigar-chewing Curtis LeMay loomed ominously in the background.

However, General LeMay's main preoccupation was his strategic bomber force, which left us mostly on our own. Schilling and I freewheeled among the avionics industry, coaxing high-ranking executives to make us free loans of "black boxes," together with their attending technicians.

The alternative was to wait for years for black boxes to roll out of the complex development cycle, and Schilling reckoned he couldn't wait that long. Therefore, by reason of my civilian status and an independent income which helps keep a man free of conflict-of-interest problems, and since I had no military career at stake, and also because I possessed the added asset of knowing my way around the aviation industrial circuit, I found myself bearing the brunt of borrowing the needed black boxes, and then personally testing them in any convenient F-84 that didn't need to be immediately available for regular missions.

Although this short-circuiting process did not endear me to various bureaucratic chieftains, I tiptoed gently enough to insure beneficial rapport with the many dedicated technical people of the Air Research and Development Command who would in the future be lending a helping hand.

I found the operating wings and squadrons of the Strategic Air Command to be models of military effectiveness, but my impressions of research and development under government auspices were less favorable. The channels of authority were oftentimes so sluggish and resistant that a well-conceived project could simply die in the pipeline from old age unless tagged with sky-high priority and assigned to a high-ranking *single manager* who could personally ramrod it through the labyrinth. This sluggishness was especially conspicuous if the idea had been born outside of, or not comfortably channeled within, the research and development complex.

The operating commands had a word for it. They called it the NIH factor—Not Invented Here.

Vice-Admiral Hyman G. Rickover had something to say about this problem during his testimony of July 25, 1968, before the Congressional Joint Committee on Atomic Energy. Here are some excerpts:

> What is basically wrong with the Defense Department, in my opinion, is the excessive size of its Headquarters. . . . The headquarters staff has become so vast that it has gone out of control of its own leaders. . . .
>
> There are so many layers of administrators that they constitute a thicket impeding action on vital matters for which Department of Defense approval must be obtained. At numerous points there are barriers— often manned by relatively minor administrators— which check progress. In consequence almost nothing can now be decided without inordinate delay. . . .
>
> It is bad enough to make wrong decisions but infinitely worse to make none at all. . . . This is a dangerous game. Our enemies will not politely hold their hand while still another study is made by the Defense Department. . . .
>
> In a homely manner of speaking, The Defense Department is constipated. It must be purged or it will become increasingly torpid.

Even more frustrating was the fear of controversy instilled in research and development management. An innocent little black box can be a source of embarrassment, and generals are unlikely to achieve their next star if they cast an approving eye on equipment which does not fall within accepted guidelines. There are times when a bona-fide concept can't even be objectively discussed in such a brainwashed environment, much less officially subjected to vigorous, searching trial.

Because of this unfortunate timidity, one of the most promising of all navigational techniques that came to my attention, a practical and proven capability developed in a friendly but foreign nation—and one which would, if thoroughly wrung out, have had an enormous *practical* impact in Vietnam in the crucial nineteen-sixties—died unwanted and unloved. (We'll come back to this later.)

One difficulty was sheer, monolithic bigness, but mainly it was the absence of a competitive spark, which won't stay lit in an oppressive atmosphere. A cure is not likely to be achieved, it seems to me, until weapons-systems development is broken up among competitive segments of the fighter and bomber commands.

Bigness, we know, has produced some remarkable weapons systems, but only when guided personally by officers of domineering rank, such as LeMay, Rickover, General Bernard Schriever, and Admiral William Raborn. Less glamorous details—the guts of what makes a weapons system work—too often are hung up in the pipeline. Navigation for instance—my own specialty—happens to be one of those details.

Despite the billions we Americans spend to find our way around in the sky, we have been living, in certain important respects, in navigational poverty. This does not mean our spending has been niggardly. In fact, too much money has been spent. The trouble can be traced to profligate expenditures for doing jobs the hard way, while other vital navigational needs are totally neglected.

Nor are the sluggish research and development pipelines entirely to blame for this unhappy state of navigational affairs. Industrial and bureaucratic politics have done even worse damage.

Despite these impressions of G.I. research and development I never had anything but a cordial relationship with my associates in the Air Force experimental establishment. In due course I grew accustomed to the bureaucratic machinery there, and became acquainted with many of the best men in fighter testing. Among them was Major General Al Boyd who did what very few generals take the time and trouble to do. He divided his time between his desk and his airplanes, and thus had firsthand knowledge of the better features, as well as the shortcomings, of the test equipment he was responsible for. He sorted out, or consigned to oblivion, many tons of glowing brochures.

My earlier visits to the WADC at Dayton, Ohio's Wright-Patterson Air Force Base, were less than auspicious. In fact, on one occasion, I was almost taken into custody.

I had come across the mountains from Georgia on a sunny spring day in 1952 in one of Schilling's F-84 single-seaters. I was clad in an ordinary business suit instead of the "man from Mars" regalia of a fighter pilot. I had habitually dropped in at various SAC bases in this offhand attire without disturbing the security apparatus. My oddest of odd jobs was well known at these places.

But it wasn't well known at the WADC. Such indifferent civilian garments were hardly to be expected on the lone occupant of a combat-ready SAC fighter.

When I laddered myself down from the cockpit onto the parking area tarmac at Wright-Patterson, a stony-faced duty officer accosted me.

The young captain was above five feet six, heavyset, and not at all cordial. "Where from?" he inquired sharply.

"From Turner" was my affable reply, though I sensed I was not among friends.

The hostile young man could not reasonably associate a SAC jet fighter with my wrinkled business suit, a garment which had looked much neater before I had donned a tight-fitting parachute. Obviously I had somehow penetrated an impenetrable base of the Strategic Air Command and pilfered a combat-ready airplane.

The situation was about to become embarrassing, and I could appreciate the young officer's befuddlement.

So I flashed my special Pentagon document. It was the only time I ever needed to.

This odd job was the only one of its kind, and it was meant to be temporary. But it wasn't. For ten years I was heavily involved in working out procedures that would put the baby supernukes where they would have their most devastating effect. I became a "delivery" specialist.

Over the years I flew almost every model of Air Force jet fighter through more than a thousand experimental hours of tinkering with the most effective techniques for finding a target and eliminating it. Even my weekend flights to Europe in charge of a Pan American Airways Stratocruiser abetted the undertaking. There was no better place than the left front seat of an ocean-hopping airliner, suspended in a sky full of stars, to sort out puzzling problems.

My skull was cluttered with "hard" and "soft" targets, and reverberated with "air bursts" and "ground bursts." This can have an effect on a man's psyche. Above all, it eliminates every last vestige of complacency about the future.

At the beginning I was still a naval reservist, but a lagging naval connection didn't last long in a zealous Air Force atmosphere. The purification process was so complete that within a few years, after pausing a while as a chicken colonel, I was admitted to the Air Force generals' "club" with the lone star of a brigadier. But I was a very junior member. There is no one lower on the general officers' totem pole than a reserve brigadier general, even though my association was with the regular, not the reserve, establishment.

This wasn't an easy club to get into. The President of the United States has the first chance to blackball. Then his preselected list of new generals goes to the Senate Armed Services Committee for approval.

These senators are the guardians of the club's portals, and one of the more vigilant sentinels happened to be a lady from Maine—Senator Margaret Chase Smith.

The senator from Maine has been known to wield a hefty shillelagh in a most unladylike manner. I was never aimed at directly, it seemed, but I felt some glancing blows. What, for instance, was this ex-naval aviator doing in the Air Force?

But the lady senator eventually relented after finding out my reason for being there. So I picked up my one-star flag along with some other amenities.

The generals were mostly an impressive lot, but there were some, as in any group anywhere, including all the military services, who weren't heavily endowed with brain-power. These underpowered gentlemen, I was unhappy to discover, created an illusion of omnipotence by simply throwing their bullheaded weight around. Their credo was "Don't confuse me with the facts." I had trouble with this kind of general.

I had one special misgiving about attaining star rank. Generals, unfortunately, aren't supposed to do much flying. Being rusty they're usually furnished with "seeing-eye" lieutenants to keep them out of trouble when they go aloft. Therefore most of my productive flying in Air Force fighters was done before I joined this august society.

In the days of the SRDC I had an F-84 assigned to our special project which became a casualty of the cold war, and it took one of my talented assistants, Lieutenant Bill Brandt, along with it. We were testing a star tracker, a photoelectric device for measuring the angularity of the stars, but we had poked so many holes in the airplane to accommodate the test equipment that something had gone wrong with the cockpit pressurization.

However, to expedite the tests, I persisted in flying the

airplane without cockpit pressure. Under these circumstances the thin air of the stratosphere can pose a dangerous problem.

During my absence on a Pan Am flight to Europe Bill Brandt took the airplane aloft from Turner on a Sunday afternoon with instructions to fly at an altitude which would assure his continued good health. His job was to track the sun with the F-84's photoelectric apparatus.

But the cloud tops were high. The eager young pilot must have chased his celestial target high above them into the menacing thin air.

Whatever happened, Brandt never came back. Our search sorties swept and reswept the southeastern United States without finding a trace.

A minor oxygen lapse could have put him to sleep. If so, the unthinking autopilot took charge and flew the sleeping aviator hundreds of miles beyond the coastline—any coastline—in the direction ordained by his last conscious steer. Eventually the engine ran dry of fuel. The robot pilot held course and altitude a few final moments. Then, with airspeed gone, the airplane fell out of the sky, straight down into the rolling blue swells. Bill Brandt would be hidden forever at the bottom of an unknown sea.

But in spite of this saddening blow, we made progress, and the fighter office in the Pentagon allocated another F-84 to be my own personal flying laboratory. This was the new model—the F—with wings swept back at a 45 degree angle. It was the Air Force's first swept-wing fighter type.

It was a beautiful airplane. I named it *Excalibur IV*, the next in lineage to my P-51 of the Arctic solo. For three years it was my own personal flying machine. I barnstormed it around the United States and even took it across the Atlantic.

Numerous holes were bored in this airplane, too, to accommodate the wiring that connected the new gadgets in the cockpit to the black boxes up forward in the gun deck.

Therefore *Excalibur IV*'s cockpit was unduly porous, and somewhat afflicted with short circuits and other nerve-racking ailments.

But it was a gadgeteer's dream. It survived many adventures which, as the following chapter will testify, were sometimes made more exciting by the profusion of its ailments.

But most of the difficulties were caused by the new and untried gadgets, and by the inadequacies of my own personal screwdriver. There was no basic fault in the airplane itself. This F84-F came off the production line of Republic Aviation, a company famed for the excellence of its fighters, and when the airplane became nonstandard, the despairing people who built it still generously supported their orphan offspring.

Still, good results were achieved, and *Excalibur IV* never killed anyone, although there were times when I thought that it might.

Command of the 31st Strategic Fighter Wing was eventually turned over to another fighter ace of World War II. Colonel Gordon Graham was in charge of the Wing when SAC discarded its fighters and transferred them to the Tactical Air Command. Graham, who is now a three-star general, and vice-commander of the Tactical Air Command, was as effective as Schilling, but his methods were different. Not as swashbuckling, he substituted some extra-vigorous brainpower for advancing the concepts we worked with. Therefore the search for new techniques and equipment flourished.

But there were times when the SRDC needed a bigger workshop than my F84-F. It couldn't accommodate all the black boxes on hand.

So I convinced Colonel Frank Ellis, commander of SAC's 44th Bomb Wing at Lake Charles in Louisiana, that one of his B-47s would make an ideal conveyance, which it did. I found that my aircraft commander's seat of this six-engine jet bomber was an effective branch office of the SRDC. We even achieved credible bomb scores by a process of tracking the stars with our photoelectric eyeballs.

While experimenting with this stargazing bomb-delivery technique I became closely associated with the brilliantly articulate Ellis, who took the trouble to convey a store of his knowledge about strategic bombing. I learned some practical lessons when I was put in charge of a segment of his bomber force on a simulated combat exercise during the Suez crisis.

Schilling, the fighter pilot, and Ellis, the bomber commander, each had a flair for ruling his realm, but each did it differently. Schilling, supported by his fighter gunnery record against the German *Luftwaffe,* ruled by spreading his contagious enthusiasm down through the ranks to the lowest airman in his outfit. Ellis, on the other hand, accepted no nonsense from anyone. He was the king of his domain, nor was this impression diminished by the vast megatonage of explosives he kept at the ready.

But the luck of these two close associates, who were always at the center of the action, took a wrong turn. Schilling's racing car hit a culvert on a winding road in England. Ellis nudged a California mountain with his B-47.

The culvert and the mountain succeeded where the guns of the enemy had tried and failed. I walked with their caissons at Arlington, each time sorrowfully aware the world of the sky had grown smaller in their absence, as had my own.

CHAPTER ELEVEN

Shark Bait

There were no overstuffed armchairs in the SRDC. This would always be an airborne think factory.

Excalibur IV, my F84-F flying lab, sometimes has a wanderlust. Therefore, on this eighteenth day of April in 1956 we're going to head eastward across the Atlantic.

This experiment has been labeled Shark Bait, a name it will almost live up to.

Shark Bait is scheduled to be the first nonstop flight of jet fighters across the Atlantic on the direct, great-circle route, and the first with only one in-flight refueling. Although it is mainly a deployment exercise to demonstrate the most rapid possible transfer of fighter aircraft to Europe, it's also a test of my airplane's newly designed guidance equipment. Therefore part of my task is to find the Wethersfield Royal Air Force Station near the east coast of England, without using radio.

The trip has another, more personal purpose. I'm nursing a furtive desire to recapture my transatlantic speed record which has been stolen again, this time by an Englishman. He pilfered it and made his getaway in a Canberra jet bomber.

But bad news can hit at the worst time and place. Our three F84-F single-seaters are at the end of the long runway at McGuire Air Force Base in the middle of New Jersey. We're ready for takeoff, and among other things, we're ready to snatch back that record.

The control tower relays an urgent message: "Shark Bait, your weather reconnaissance advises that cloud tops in Area One are too high for refueling operations. You will rendezvous with tankers in Area Two."

I hide a perplexed grimace behind my oxygen mask. Where in this weather-bedeviled world is Area Two? None of us has ever heard of it. In our briefing with the tanker people three weeks ago it was agreed that alternate refueling areas would be spelled out in plain English. Meanwhile some bright-eyed young super-spook has dreamed up a secret scheme which includes a mysteriously coded *Area Two*. But he didn't bother to tell us the code.

The computer inside my skull spins a torrent of numbers. The whole plan of action must be rehashed within a matter of seconds, and the diversely complicated considerations are not easy to sort out. We're already two weeks behind schedule, and behind us is the momentum generated by weeks of heavy preparation. As Shark Bait leader I must decide right now whether or not to cancel the mission.

Shall we taxi meekly back with our tail between our legs to wait for a better weather situation? Shall we struggle all over again with a clutter of badly conceived regulations which have shackled us to the ground while the weather along the route has been invitingly favorable?

With no doubt in my mind I sound off into my oxygen

mask, "McGuire tower from Shark Bait. We're ready to roll."

"Cleared for takeoff. Left turn out" crackles into my helmet.

I glance to my right at Tomlinson, to the left at Martinez. They're full of the bad news and they're glaring fiercely from under their hard hats and oxygen masks. I can only see their eyes, but there's no need to talk. Their eyes say, "Let's go." The vote is three to nothing.

The charge of a bull elephant is not easy to stop. Neither is the charge of a herd of fighter jockeys who are tuned up to go.

We'll solve the mystery of Area Two while pressing on toward Newfoundland. If we can't find those tankers, there are places to land along the way.

My right hand gesticulates engine run-up. With my left I thrust the throttle forward. Tomlinson and Martinez nod their readiness. Together the three airplanes surge along the asphalt to a hundred and seventy-five knots and pull free, accelerating in a climbing left turn toward the northeast. At four hundred and fifty knots we settle into close formation to cruise low and fast across the flat New Jersey farmlands under a ceiling of gray-bottomed stratus clouds.

Sandy Hook is sighted ahead and slightly to the left; to the right are the Jersey beaches. As we approach the south shore of Brooklyn the low clouds offer big breaks. We find a big hole and poke our collective noses into the blue sky above New York's big airport at Idlewild. The control tower checks our time of crossing just in case we set that transatlantic speed record.

At thirty-five thousand feet we're leveled off, and I engage my autopilot. *Excalibur IV*'s whirling jet turbine bores energetically through the sky. I look back at my wing men a few moments and admire the long, vaporous contrails streaming from their tailpipes.

But there's no time to waste. We must solve that tanker mystery. "Area Two" must be translated into unmistakable English.

I give this job to Martinez. He drops back into loose formation and shifts radio frequency.

I get busy with my special navigational devices. My direction-finding radio will be deactivated to make the navigation test more realistic, but Tomlinson and Martinez will keep their "bird dogs" tuned in for extra safety. But they'll say nothing unless we go conspicuously astray.

Excalibur IV's star tracker, together with its small-size Doppler radar, makes my special F-84 independent of any navigational assistance from the earth's surface. The airplane will be guided by measuring the angularity of the sun and stars, and by the probing electronic fingers of the Doppler radar which bounces its signals off the earth to reckon groundspeed and drift.

Although my radio direction finder has been sealed by safety wire in the *off* position, it can be brought back to life with a wire cutter. I happen to have one. It cost me $1.87 secondhand, which could be a bargain. But my reputation will suffer if I use it.

A glance over the right side reveals a curved tentacle of land immersed in a calm, windless ocean. Cape Cod is the last landmark we'll see in North America. But it soon disappears. A curtain of cloud rolls underneath.

Martinez is back on our radio frequency. He has a report.

"Colonel," he barks crisply. "Nobody can explain Area Two. It's a secret. All I got was the weather, and it's getting worse. Torbay is down to a hundred-foot ceiling with a quarter-mile visibility. Gander has four hundred and a half in fog. Harmon is good."

We can be thankful the weather isn't a secret. Otherwise, being classified, we're as untouchable as a snake. Nobody wants to know us.

One reason for our being in this secret strait jacket today can be traced to the last time a flight of F84-Fs was launched on a transatlantic exercise. Three of the four airplanes didn't survive the takeoff, nor did the pilots.

As a result, from the moment this expedition was conceived, we have been smothered with regulations which cover every fanciful problem. Until today we've been governed by inconsequential weather details. Now, after being submerged to our ears in unneeded advice, we find ourselves launched into the worst kind of weather.

I contemplate the problem: Torbay in southeast Newfoundland near St. John's and Gander in the north will be the closest emergency airports if we should miss connections with the tankers. But a warm front which should have moved far to the east of Newfoundland has reversed itself—a rare occurrence—and now sits squarely over Torbay, Gander, and our original refueling area one hundred miles east-northeast of Torbay.

If we fly as far east as Torbay to search for the tankers, and don't find them, we'll not have enough fuel to return to Harmon Air Force Base at Stephensville in southwest Newfoundland. A southwesterly jet stream blowing across Newfoundland will guarantee that. Yet, if we turn around short of Torbay, we'll never find out where the tankers went.

Yarmouth, in Nova Soctia, lies twenty miles ahead under the clouds, according to the star tracker which is taking measure of the sun. Wind? True speed? It's all on the dials in front of me. The Doppler radar shows we're making five hundred and forty knots—nine nautical miles each minute. That means it's approximately two minutes to Yarmouth. I jot this down on my clipboard.

But navigational details right now are a distracting annoyance. My head is full of the big question. Where on this cloud-ridden planet are our flying gas stations? I'm hoping the radar station at Torbay will give us a clue when we're close enough to talk to them. Then, if Area Two turns out to be beyond reach, we'll drop in at Gander.

But the worsening weather at Gander is anything but a tranquil thought. That Newfoundland outpost is closing in under a blanket of drizzle and fog. Stopping there would require a downwind formation landing out of a low ceiling and poor visibility onto a wet, slippery runway, touching down at a hundred and forty knots of airspeed, and with no drag chutes to help slow us down. There would be no margin for a slight miscalculation, or the wrong kind of luck.

The weather at Harmon is wide open and inviting, but a landing there would be a victory for the headshakers. Certainly we would never be allowed to try this journey another time. The logic of a direct flight to Europe with the simplest possible refueling arrangements would lose its credibility. So would the navigational concepts we're working on.

Fighter aircraft, as a rule, have been crossing the Atlantic on the warm-weather route via Bermuda and the Azores, air-refueling from tankers several times along the way. The other choice has been a roundabout trip by way of Labrador, Greenland, and Iceland.

We're also pursuing the idea that a future, grown-up version of this swift-strike fighter can take over part of the big bomber's role, and do certain jobs at less cost, and with more speed and agility. The small-size navigational boxes up forward in *Excalibur*'s nose are a step along the way.

But it appears that Lady Luck isn't bestowing any favors around Newfoundland today. This eccentric warm front up ahead—this rare breed of back-pedaling weather—must have joined a conspiracy to stop us.

Still, that erratic warm front isn't as much of an obstacle as the crippling memorandum full of inept rules and regulations which bogged us down at McGuire. I have unpleasant memories of the excellent route weather we were obliged to pass up because some inconsequential alternate destination wasn't enjoying its sunniest skies. For example, the weather at Burtonwood, near Liverpool, was less than perfect four days in a row. But conditions at Burtonwood, on the opposite side of England from our destination beyond London, were of little significance when inspected by a practiced weather eye.

These unnecessary delays have driven us against a cut-off deadline and an irreversible commitment. Therefore, we'll not land short of London tonight, except as a last resort.

I'm sure that Tomlinson and Martinez feel just as assertive as I. Both are fiercely competitive fighter pilots. Major Robert C. (Tommy) Tomlinson, on my right wing, is from the Air Force fighter operations office where I work in the Pentagon. Tomlinson has flown jet fighters as much as anyone, anywhere.

On my left wing is Captain Cesar (Jose) Martinez, Operations Officer of the 509th Fighter-Bomber Squadron at Langley Air Force Base in Virginia. A million-miler in jet fighters, he's observing this transatlantic exercise firsthand on behalf of the Tactical Air Command.

These are the best kind of military pilots, the sort who are more interested in maximum performance than in maximum assurance they'll collect their old age pensions.

I return to my electronic devices. The celestial tracker feeds out some meaningful digits. Nova Scotia, blanketed by cloud, has been invisible its full length from Yarmouth to Sydney, and now the tracker shows it's behind us. The Doppler groundspeed meter, its reading steadily increasing, reveals we've entered the swift current of a jet stream. It creeps up to six hundred knots, which means we're hurtling toward our ambiguous tanker rendezvous at nearly seven hundred miles an hour, crabbing to the right to maintain our intended track while riding the torrent of wind. At this rate we'll soon be within talking distance of the Torbay radar station.

The layer of clouds below remains unbroken and builds up to higher altitudes on the eastern horizon. These higher clouds are the backside of the erratic warm front. We must refuel above them—but can we? The tops may be too high for our tankers, handicapped by their old-fashioned piston engines.

Twenty minutes from Torbay, close enough for radio contact, I thumb the throttle mike button and fire the pregnant question, "Torbay, this is Shark Bait. Got any tankers around?"

The swift answer gives our hopes a new chill. "Shark Bait, your refuelers last reported two hundred and thirty miles east-northeast of this station, heading east. They've disappeared from my crystal ball."

Our fueling stations are far at sea, beyond our point of no return, even beyond the vision of ground radar which must bring us together. Those long, dry runways at Harmon are beckoning. A quick turn, a long dive, and we could snuggle back to Mother Earth. But there's still a fighting chance if the tankers can be brought back.

"Turn 'em around!"

My message carries far out over the Atlantic. A faint acknowledgment seems to come from another world. "Roger Shark Bait" filters through my earphones. The tankers, hundreds of miles away, have heard us.

The radarman at Torbay sounds off with an urgent order: "Tankers, reverse course to Torbay. Climb at war-emergency power to twenty-thousand." But it is unlikely the distant tanker men can hear a message from the ground.

Yet *my* message was heard. The tankers must surely be turning back toward Newfoundland. But I'm not dead sure. I go on the air again: "Shark Bait tankers, confirm reversing course." No answer! I try again—I hear nothing!

That dry concrete at Harmon is now beyond reach,

literally gone with the wind. We're riding in the core of the jet stream, with just enough fuel left to fly a hundred and fifty miles beyond the Newfoundland shoreline, and turn back—if we miss the tankers—to fog-smitten Gander.

If the tankers have reversed course, the gap between us is closing at fourteen miles each minute. But how far at sea are the tankers? Perhaps too far. I put the question over the air.

"Stand by," comes the answer from Torbay.

Torbay radar has spotted us, still to the west of his station. We're advised to "steer ninety degrees," although the tankers have not yet reappeared on the radarman's scope.

The unbroken expanse of clouds beneath us is now darkened ahead by higher layers. The stratification appears to merge as we approach the warm front, leaving no clear room between cloud layers for refueling. Flying at thirty-five thousand feet, we ride out to sea on a tenuous hope, continually thinking about Gander and the low ceiling there.

I take another reading on the Doppler and celestial tracker. The celestial device shows that we passed Torbay at 1920 Greenwich Mean Time, one hour, fifty-three and a half minutes after passing over New York, now eleven hundred and fifty miles behind our tailpipes.

Directly below us, near the tall cliffs at Cape Race, the radarmen of the Air Defense Command are just beginning to warm up for the afternoon's exercise. Hunched over the radarscope is the Intercept Controller, First Lieutenant Bill Romaine, whose radio chatter is brisk and full of authority. For the next hour Romaine will be "flying" with those blips on his scope. It is his job to put the tankers and fighters together, guiding us astern of the tankers much as he would guide fighters to the intercept of enemy bombers.

Such a maneuver is routine enough when the weather is good. But it's not so easy when the sky is cluttered with frontal clouds, especially when the tankers can't fly above them. Even worse, the tankers have disappeared off the edge of the Torbay radar. Only one big blip remains, which is Shark Bait racing across an otherwise deserted radar-scope.

Romaine, no doubt, wishes there were a sky hook for that fast-moving blip to hang on to. It would be helpful if we could dangle in midair without burning any fuel while awaiting the tankers' return. But in the absence of such an unheard-of contrivance, we can't linger for a moment. If we're to land in England tonight we must hold course to the east and tap the tankers on the first pass. If we find them in time.

Suddenly something is stirring at the top of Romaine's crystal ball. It's a big blip which inches slowly toward the center of the scope.

Lieutenant Romaine comes back on the air, his voice triumphant. "Shark Bait, I have your tankers on my weapon. Steer ninety-five degrees—one–one–five miles."

Our luck has turned for the better. The tanker formation, heavy with fuel, is plodding back toward Torbay against the powerful westerly.

The radar pickup comes just in time. Moments later our fuel gauges tell us there can be no turning back. Now we're irrevocably committed to getting fuel from those tankers, and that's easier said than done.

But we'll be in good shape if the cloud tops don't get in the way. We would prefer to refuel at fifteen thousand feet, where the tankers can give us enough airspeed, but the clouds are much higher than that. At twenty thousand feet, with the tankers flying at their best possible speed, we'll barely hang onto the refueling booms, our tiny wings close to a stall.

We drop down to thirty thousand, dead on track for an intercept. There is more radar guidance from Romaine. Fifteen miles to our aerial gas stations, one minute to go. I alter course a few degrees so that the tankers will pass on our left, and search the cloud tops below. My wingmen draw in close.

"Tallyho!"

To the left and far below I catch sight of four big airplanes lumbering westward. Occasionally they fly through the cloud tops and momentarily disappear. There's no time to waste.

"Dive brakes!"

Excalibur IV shudders as the dive brakes extend. We dive steeply, turning in close formation to chase the tankers' tails. Then we spread out, each of us directly behind a tanker. There is one tanker for each jet, plus a spare.

My altimeter reads twenty-one thousand feet. This won't be an easy hook-up. I lower my flaps slightly so that the airplane will handle better at slow speeds. At the flick of a switch the boom receptacle in my left wing pops open.

The tanker commander asks us what airspeed we desire. I reply, shaving a few knots off the amount we'd like to have, but still asking for more than the tankers can comfortably give us. These fuel-heavy KC-97s simply won't fly efficiently at this altitude. I'm sure of this because I've had thousands of hours at the controls of similar airplanes, the Boeing Stratocruisers of Pan American Airways.

My tanker occasionally disappears as it plunges through the clouds. I follow closely, boring in for the connection, and a glance at my fuel gauge lends a sense of urgency. I snuggle under the tanker's tail. The receptacle in my wing yawns invitingly at the tanker's long, slender boom.

In a window under the big ship's tail I can see the lad who will maneuver the boom. He regards me glumly and finally speaks up, "Back five."

I drop back. He stabs his boom into *Excalibur IV*'s left wing. The fuel gauge, a depressing sight a few moments ago, creeps up to a higher reading. It's a new lease on life.

Up front of us, the tanker pilots of the Strategic Air Command are flogging their over-revved engines at maximum boost in an all-out effort to fly faster than our minimum speed. We must find lower cloud tops, somehow, so that the tankers can descend and save their engines—but the cloud tops become higher. Soon we're entirely submerged in the milky mist—four tankers and three fighters in close formation. We hang onto the booms like suckling calves.

We had reversed course toward the west while diving down to join the tankers. Now the tanker leader orders a turn toward the north where he hopes to find lower clouds. As we turn, my airplane separates from the tanker's boom.

With my left hand I try to press the button which will rearm the circuits of the refueling receptacle in the left wing. But I discover that the fingers of this hand, my throttle hand, have been congealed by the cold steel of the throttle which I have been jockeying to maintain precise formation under the tanker's tail. The fingers of this hand are crippled and lifeless. They no longer have the strength to press even a mere button.

While cruising at thirty-five thousand feet the outside air temperature at 70 degrees below zero has cold-soaked the throttle quadrant. Totally preoccupied as I've been with flying close to the tanker's tail, I've hardly noticed the chill of the metal where my throttle hand has been resting. So now my fingers will be useless until I thaw them out.

This would be an unlikely problem in any other airplane of this type. It just happens that *Excalibur IV* is peculiar. Something has bewitched the cockpit temperature control ever since I installed the special navigation equipment. On one occasion, while cruising leisurely across Texas, the temperature control, accidentally and without being touched, went *full hot*. The cockpit became a furnace! The heat could not be shut off.

But Bergstrom Air Force Base was close by. I landed soon enough to escape from the oven.

But I don't relish this happening over the ocean. Therefore, the cockpit temperature control has been set at "full cold" where it can't cause any big trouble.

"Full hot" would give me three options today. I could ditch my speedy little flying machine in the rolling ocean, or I could bail out and sail home in the one-man dinghy which is attached to my parachute. Or, if reluctant to take such extreme measures, I could sit here and absorb the heat until I become a moistureless cadaver.

Gloves would have helped in the cold of the stratosphere. But to me they're too often a clumsy encumbrance. Therefore I stowed them away.

It won't be healthy to remove my right hand from the control stick. The tail of the tanker is only a few feet above. The air is choppy.

But there's no other choice. Certainly I can't press that button with my big toe, and if nothing presses it *Excalibur IV* won't be getting another drop of fuel. The airplane will fall out of the sky into an ocean which is not recommended for swimming.

My right hand darts across the cockpit to the tantalizing button, which puts me quickly back in the refueling business. *Excalibur IV*, momentarily unguided, prances a little. The boom operator in the tanker's window looks unhappy. But there's no use cluttering up the airwaves explaining my problem.

Maybe that lad doesn't relish having the higher-ranking types fly so close to his tail. Colonels are usually so submerged in paper work they seldom get out for refueling practice.

I did not neglect the practice. But rehearsing at a sedate fifteen thousand feet, over land, in smooth air, with two hands, is different. And we didn't practice *inside* the clouds.

So it's not the same today, and the worst problem is the airspeed. These piston-engine tankers can't give us enough up here at twenty-one thousand feet where they're flying on instruments in the bumpy cloud tops.

❁

On top of that, the fuel gauge is beginning to look anemic again; one hand is almost out of action, and I'm vaguely aware that the sharks down below are gazing fondly skyward.

If my good friend in aviation insurance, Thom Shea, could see me now, he'd never fix me up with another nickel's worth of life insurance.

This area around Newfoundland has snagged me before. During a 1942 visit to Gander in the flying boat *Excalibur I* it was a load of ice that gave us trouble. The heavily iced wing-tip floats shook so violently they appeared on the verge of tearing loose. Luckily only the pitot mast carried away before we escaped in the direction of Shediac.

Nor was the speed dash to London in my P-51 *Excalibur III* an easy affair while in this part of the world. Starved of oxygen that time, I became a witless derelict in the Newfoundland sky, blown out to sea on the crest of a jet stream.

We're not doing much better today. I jockey back into position, and the boom thuds back into *Excalibur IV*'s receptacle. The spot on the tanker I must line up so carefully is now out of sight behind the metal frame which separates my cockpit canopy from the windshield. Being too tall for this cockpit I slide forward in my seat until I'm almost lying down to get a better view. The angle is anything but comfortable.

Exactly a week ago in this vicinity I was relaxing at an easygoing angle in the captain's chair of a Pan Am Stratocruiser, with my feet propped up below the instrument panel, griping at the stewardess because the hot chocolate wasn't just right. Today, by contrast, my desires are at rock bottom. I'm only interested in basic essentials, such as a full load of fuel, and I'd like it fast.

On the airlines, where we take great care to render maximum safety and comfort, it's not customary to fly in this fashion. But today, conducting a searching military exercise, the safety and comfort factors are balanced against the gains we hope to achieve.

My headphones reveal that Tommy and Jose are fully fueled and standing by. My tanks should be full to the top, too, but the fuel gauge has stopped at the three-quarter mark. The boom operator announces, "I've got pressure but no flow." Something has gone wrong in *Excalibur IV*'s fuel system.

I disconnect from the boom and draw back a few yards to investigate the difficulty. A check of the individual fuel gauges tells me the right-hand external pylon is still empty. It's a large four hundred and fifty gallon tank; I can't reach the other side of the Atlantic unless it's filled.

A tiny fuel valve is stuck in the closed position. Jose suggests that I pull a certain circuit breaker which will by-pass the electrical signal from the closed valve. The circuit-breaker panel is somewhere near my right foot, out of sight. Keeping an eye on my tanker, I bend forward and blindly run my hand along the surface of the panel, feeling for the second row from the top, fourth circuit breaker from the front. I find the button and pull it out, but the effect is not what I wanted; my refueling receptacle slams shut. It appears that my airplane, an earlier model than Jose's, is wired differently.

I reset the little button to reopen the wing receptacle, and go back on the tanker boom for another connection. It's no good. The boom operator repeats, "Pressure but no flow."

I consider the problem. We have enough fuel now to fly all the way back to Harmon in southwest Newfoundland. Or we can proceed farther out to sea with the tankers, re-fuel to the maximum again, and continue east. I can land at Shannon, in Ireland, and thus complete the navigational testing phase of the trip, in spite of my empty tank. My wingmen can take leave of me over Shannon and fly on to England to complete the deployment exercise. It won't be ideal, scattering ourselves in this way, but the job will be done. The speed record has gone down the drain, but it hardly rates a passing thought. We've been too busy just keeping those sharks down below from enjoying a good meal.

I wonder about that. These rubber exposure suits we're wearing might not be the tastiest of all dishes to a sleekly finned ocean-going gourmet. I ponder that this may be the best reason of all for wearing such clumsy apparatus. Otherwise, it seems to me, this bulky "moon" suit made of rubber armor is more hazardous than protective.

At first I thought the tight neckband would strangle me before we could reach England, but ever since takeoff I've been too busy even to realize I'm wearing it. Now I'm beginning to think better of my awkward garb. The ocean east of Newfoundland is freezing cold and full of ominous-looking ice floes.

No one thinks seriously of returning to fog-soaked Newfoundland. The tanker commander agrees to escort us out to sea. He takes an east-northeasterly heading, pointing toward distant Ireland, and we fly awkwardly at slow speed in the wake of the tankers toward our jumping-off point. I rework the fuel-versus-mileage computation. At what point can we take leave of the tankers? If we stay with them too long we'll compromise certain important requirements of the mission. If we leave too soon, I'll be shark bait for sure. I estimate the shortened range of my airplane, allowing for the empty fuel tank, and mentally spread the figures across the miles from our present position to Shannon. My figures are padded slightly by reckoning zero tailwind, and I add a few hundred pounds of fuel for unforeseen problems. This will be my reserve fuel over Shannon.

But our plans are jolted momentarily by a new development. Jose has oxygen trouble. A valve has unseated, causing his entire supply of liquid oxygen to vent overboard.

Does he wish to return to Newfoundland? He growls a "Negative," which suggests he resents the idea.

Without oxygen for Jose, we must fly lower than planned, and that will increase the rate of fuel consumption. I revise my fuel and navigational figures, reckoning a jumping-off point readjusted to the airplane's pressurized-cabin altitude. Jose should be able to function safely with his cockpit at a pressure altitude of twelve thousand feet. What does he think?

"No sweat," he advises, and raises the figure to fourteen thousand. Allowing for the pressure in his cockpit, that will give us a cruising altitude near thirty-five thousand feet. For an emergency, Jose has a few minutes of oxygen attached to his parachute in a jump bottle.

Down in the radar shack at Cape Race it has been a difficult afternoon for Lieutenant Romaine and the sixteen men who support him. (His letter a few months later had this to say: "I, too, 'flew' Operation Shark Bait. When you and the tankers left my scope outbound I was dripping with perspiration. It was even running down the channels at the rear of my anklebone. Colonel Riggs, who sat next to me monitoring the air-ground frequencies, came into the Operations building looking like a fashion-plate-type colonel. Before it was over he had his blouse off, tie off, sleeves up, hair rumpled, and he, too, was dripping wet.")

The cloud tops are lowering as we fly toward the east behind the tankers. We ease down to seventeen thousand feet. My left hand has by now thawed out, and I maneuver behind a tanker to try my luck again. Down here at a lower altitude the hook-up is much easier, but the fuel-gauge needle still stops short at the three-quarter mark, just as before. I disconnect and try again.

Suddenly there's a warning shout from the boom operator: "Receiver, you're siphoning fuel!"

The vital liquid is flowing overboard in a thick stream from the main-tank fuel vent. It's another stuck valve—

this time the shut-off valve in the top of my main fuselage tank. I grope hastily in the region of my left foot to pull the battle-damage switches. The overflow stops.

An air-sea-rescue amphibian happens to be circling below us. It calls itself Duckbutt Whisky. Its appearance here was prearranged weeks ago. Maybe we were psychic to pick this spot.

Hoping to cure my sticky valves, I draw away from the tanker and shake the airplane violently, pulling several times the force of gravity. Then I go back for another thrust of the tanker's boom. The needle of the fuel gauge reverses its downward direction, and rises steadily to *full*. There's no siphoning. Tommy and Jose are simultaneously topping off. We break away with full tanks, suddenly cured of the big difficulty.

"Good luck," says the tanker commander as he signs off. His four double-deckers bank into a sweeping turn on their way back to Newfoundland.

At full throttle we climb to thirty-two thousand feet. It's a new flight. Two thousand miles to go. We cruise at maximum speed with engine compressors spinning at 96 percent of their limit. Jose, without oxygen, must be expedited.

Cirrus clouds lend a gray cast to the western sky as the sun drops below the horizon. The insignia which adorns Jose's fuselage glistens in the fading light. It is the skull and rose of the 509th Fighter-Bomber Squadron, 405th Wing of the Tactical Air Command; Martinez is the squadron commander's right-hand man. He is an undiluted fighter pilot who logs only single-engine, single-seat flying time. Jose reckons this is the only kind of flying worth counting.

Tomlinson's airplane is the glossiest. Fresh from the factory, it is the latest model F84-F with some extra thrust in its engine. Tommy is well known among fighter pilots, having eliminated some Messerschmitts from the sky over Italy back in World War II. More recently he led the Skyblazer fighter acrobatic team in Europe. Nowadays he's not so exuberant about his desk in the Pentagon.

We cross the 35th meridian of west longitude and pull up to thirty-six thousand five hundred feet. Jose announces his pressurized cockpit altitude indicates fourteen thousand feet. We'll go no higher.

The black night surrounds us with a canopy of stars. Directly astern is the planet Venus, hanging like a lantern in the western sky. The lens of the star tracker has an electronic lock on Venus, measuring her for precise data which tell us of our progress across the meridians.

I keep glancing to right and left to make sure Tommy and Jose are still out there and reasonably close. It's not a good idea to spread out too far at night and risk becoming separated. But these fighter pros stay where they belong, appearing to hang in space, their red and green navigation lights blinking against the backdrop of stars. Occasionally Tommy and I chat a little, mostly about Jose's problem. Without oxygen, he's saving his breath.

Suddenly Jose's radio comes alive with another problem.

"I've got trouble with my pee-tube," he complains. "Can't make the connection. My zipper's stuck."

Tommy cuts in. "When you gotta go, you gotta go."

"How about it, Colonel?"

"Permission granted."

A minute later I call back. "Shark Bait Two. How's it going?"

"Gone, sir."

I have stray thoughts about fighter aircraft traveling in the regular formation of four, rather than three. We are one short, and if the ghost of a fourth airplane should join up to fly along with us, the man I would most like to see would be Bill Brandt, my young assistant at Turner Air Force Base who was lost while testing the original model of the star-tracking device now mounted in *Excalibur IV*'s nose.

But Bill couldn't make it. He's probably strapped in his airplane somewhere on the bottom of the ocean.

The star tracker casts Venus aside at my bidding and starts measuring Polaris, a faint pinpoint of light in the northern sky. The North Star guides us due east as we cling to a latitude a few miles south of the 53rd parallel. I pick up the sextant and shoot the star Arcturus, which glistens high over the nose, telling us we're passing the 30th meridian of west longitude. We've left mid-ocean astern.

Since we left the tankers I've had no more problems with *Excalibur IV*. I resolve not to poke any more holes in it, or further complicate the electrical system.

The airplane has good reason to be temperamental. It is probably the first jet ever to be barnstormed. An orphan of the skies, it has had only the most casual connection with any tactical unit.

Keeping this stray airplane mechanically fit has not been easy. When I first contemplated making this flight across the Atlantic, it seemed prudent to drop in at the Republic factory at Farmingdale for an inspection of the engine. One look at the hot section verified it was near the point of disintegration. Therefore *Excalibur IV* couldn't fly again until the 509th at Langley was able to deliver a new engine, which it did after giving me a few bad moments wondering if anyone would really come to the rescue.

But right now everything in the airplane is working as it should. The engine is running smoothly, and the only discordant note is the air-conditioning system which habitually whirs and screeches like a banshee.

I look behind me to the right. Tommy is where I expect to find him. I check the left side. Jose is not there.

"Shark Bait Two from Shark Bait One—what's your position?" No answer. Tommy calls Jose. All we hear is silence. I search the northern sky for his blinking lights but can see only a black void filled with stars. Suddenly a dark specter swoops up from below. It's Jose, waving his multicolored flashlight to say he's all right. His radio has gone dead.

We're coming up on the coast of Ireland and are due for a report of the English weather from a specially arranged weather service. Colonel Bill Ritchie of the 20th Tactical Fighter Wing at Wethersfield is flying one of his airplanes in circles around London, high enough to top the curvature of the earth between us. From long distance he can warn us of any weather difficulty which might have turned up to the east of London. We'll have no fuel for loitering. Two circuits of the airdrome would dry up our tanks.

I've forgotten the weather ship's call sign so I sound off, "Ritchie from Shark Bait."

A familiar voice replies from faraway England, "Hey, Charlie, pull up your anchor." Ritchie is rubbing in my naval upbringing. But he has a point. I *did* have the anchor out for a while.

We fly over Shannon in the south of Ireland. Tommy ventures his opinion of the Atlantic, which, being astern, is now harmless. "Piece of cake," he says.

I suggest a small amendment to his verdict, "Pretty crumby cake around Newfoundland."

We cross the Irish Sea to find a sparkling-clear night over England. A glittering patchwork of lights decorates the black surface of the earth. Swansea, Cardiff, Bristol go by. But the great city of London outdazzles them all. The English weather is so hospitable it looks as though it's trying to compensate for the villainous clouds on the other side of the Atlantic.

We fly over London six and a half hours from New York, fifty minutes late because of that baffling melee east of Newfoundland. Our haven at Wethersfield is only fifty miles away.

Tommy and Jose could have been here forty minutes earlier, with fifteen minutes chopped off the transatlantic jet record. But, being ingrained with air discipline as good troops always are, they stood by east of Newfoundland without complaining while I gnashed my teeth in frustration and struggled with the mechanical mysteries of my electronically cluttered, over-gadgeted flying machine.

Four years later the Atlantic jet record would fall into my lap accidentally. Pan Am's Flight 114 in a Boeing 707 would get some unsolicited propulsion from a lusty winter jet stream on the way from New York to Paris. A little extra throttle would help the tailwind nail the record down.

We'd be having caviar in the cockpit, but it would have tasted a lot better if Tommy and Jose could have been there to join in the action.

But seven hundred miles an hour wouldn't be good enough for sewing up the speed record very long. Not long afterward a supersonic B-58 bomber of the Air Force would raise the ante to a thousand miles an hour, which would chop all Atlantic blue ribbons into small fragments.

The muscles of those military afterburners are getting too big for mere individuals to contend with. So I won't be trying again.

But *Excalibur IV* has had a good fling, and managed to score a few points.

A red light flickers on the instrument panel—the low-level fuel warning. It suggests we'd better get our wheels down on the ground.

But the red light doesn't raise any pulse rate. It makes no difference now. Two long rows of runway lights are beckoning, and we hear a welcoming voice: "Shark Bait from Wethersfield. Come on down. Your steak's on the fire."

"Make mine rare," says Tommy as we go barreling down through the black English night.

CHAPTER TWELVE

Trouble in a Black Box

Another long-distance fighter exercise three years later served to wipe out some lingering doubts I gathered during the refueling of Shark Bait. By this time flying the ocean in jet fighters had become routine, made more harmonious by improved airborne radar, better communications, and most of all by giving the tankers jet engines.

Excalibur IV was retired in 1958, and my affections have shifted to another *Excalibur*, number five, a North American F-100F, otherwise known as a Supersabre.

On this seventh day of August 1959, *Excalibur V*, together with a sister ship named *Pole Cat*, is scheduled to depart from Wethersfield Royal Air Force Station on the outskirts of London, the same airdrome which received the Shark Bait flight so hospitably at midnight a few years before.

The two aircraft have been down in Italy these past six

weeks doing some navigation test work. Now they're scheduled to be flown to California for reassignment to the Far East Air Force.

In deference to our recent Italian hosts we adopted the code name "Julius Caesar" for the whole test exercise, including today's journey which is slated to be the first flight of jet fighters across the Arctic Ocean. In fact, we're going all the way to the top—to the North Geographic Pole—and then to Alaska.

Besides being a ferry flight, the trip will be a route survey to test the possibilities of transferring tactical fighters across the Arctic regions. If the northern route appears feasible it might someday be a good way to transfer fighter-bombers from Europe to the Far East—or vice versa—in less than a day.

However, the deployment route wouldn't normally reach as far north as the geographic pole. We have an extra reason for going all the way to the top. Along with us are a pair of navigation computers that need testing—computers which automatically solve the problem of where an airplane has been and where it is going. In *Pole Cat* the electronic brain is a large, expensive model. In my aircraft there's a small one, simpler and much less costly. I'm betting the little one will do the job better.

The black boxes we've been testing in Italy have no business in the Arctic today. They have been left behind.

Our airplanes have supersonic speed if need be, but we'll not use it. Supersonic flying gulps too much fuel and we must fly four thousand seven hundred and thirty-five miles nonstop. Although there's only one engine, this model of fighter has two seats. A copilot makes it easier. We can spread out the work.

My companions are all F-100 experts. Captain Bob Titus, who flies *Pole Cat*, is well known as a fighter test pilot. He is from the Air Force Flight Test Center at Edwards Air Force Base in California. He's also a gunnery expert. In Vietnam, several years hence, he would distinguish himself by downing three MIGs with his Phantom II.

Captain Al Kucher, who flies with me, is from the Far East Air Force. He is from Japan, as is First Lieutenant George Wooddy who flies copilot for Titus. Kucher and Wooddy are from front-line tactical fighter outfits in the Far East.

My copilot, Al Kucher, won't be around another year. Next summer he would eject from his stricken low-flying F-100 to fall on a Japanese hillside, his chute failing to open in time.

Nor would our project test pilot in Italy, Captain Jack Mayo, survive another year of fighter testing. His F-105 would disappear over the Gulf of Mexico during a supersonic gun-firing test.

Colonel Jay Robbins, a fighter ace of World War II and commander of the USAF's 20th Tactical Fighter Wing at Wethersfield, has wished us luck. This sunny summer afternoon in England finds us overdressed, prepared as we are to become Arctic pedestrians if an engine should quit. However, the need for these awkward exposure suits has been no burden to our spirits. This should be a good trip, and we're enthusiastic about the prospect. Still, it's the kind of journey that doesn't look easy at the start.

I jam myself in the front seat of the lead aircraft. Captain Kucher, in the back seat, does the same. We're scheduled to inhabit this cage for nine hours and thirty-one minutes—so says the flight plan.

As we taxi, a matter-of-fact voice from the Wethersfield tower rattles our helmet earphones with an airways clearance. "Julius Caesar, you are cleared to Eielson Air Force Base via flight-plan route. Climb out on a heading of three-three-three." The man in the tower could easily be stifling a yawn, the clearance sounds that simple. We might just as well be hopping up to Sculthorpe, a hundred miles away.

That so-called "flight-plan route" calls for certain special arrangements. We'll be meeting our refueling tankers in midair over some remote places, north of Iceland, and again north of Greenland. There should be a last drink of fuel directly over the Pole. The timing of each rendezvous today must be absolutely precise.

Our two F-100s taxi together to the far end of the runway, where we blast away with the engine run-up. My engine power gauge sticks, but a bang with the fist frees it. The needle swings around, indicating there is plenty of power. An outboard movement of the throttle causes the afterburner to erupt and give a gratifying shove. The fires roar noisily in our tailpipes as we lift off at 13:53 plus thirty-five seconds on the Greenwich clock. The next stop is Alaska.

Anglia Control dictates a flight level of twenty-eight thousand, five hundred feet until we're beyond their jurisdiction. England's small size calls for densely packed airways. The traffic control will loosen up after we've passed the Arctic Circle. We're soon past Prestwick, Scotland, and are pushing along at fair speed in the teeth of a stiff quartering headwind. I gaze down on the rugged land of my ancestors without giving them much of a thought, and then rummage around in the cockpit for my sun compass. I'll keep our gyros honest with this celestial gadget. I gave Titus one just like it. These instruments cost me $14.95 each, war surplus, the price being inflated a couple of dollars in the eight years since my P-51 journey, but still less expensive than the most insignificant rivet in this airplane.

I'm unhappy to discover that one of the reference marks for alignment of the sun-compass mount has somehow disappeared. This causes a brief scare, but a big flurry of calibrating the mount by eyeballing it makes the final setting as accurate as it needs to be.

Before making the fix I grumble about the problem through the intercom.

"That's great," says Al Kucher.

This teaches me to stop grousing into the intercom. There's no use disturbing my companion with problems he can do nothing about.

Now that the device is fixed I practice steering by the sun until it comes easy. Later on, over Greenland and the polar regions, a mistake could cause a lot of trouble.

Titus maintains a healthy separation whenever he practices his sun steering. When he's not busy with this task he sometimes flies closely alongside where the glistening beauty of his plane is highlighted in the rays of the descending sun. A polecat decorates the nose, its impudent countenance staring out from behind a barber pole. A bushy black and white tail coils possessively around the pole, significantly, we hope.

After leaving the Scottish control zone, we climb to thirty-five thousand feet but immediately drop back down a few thousand feet when the slowing groundspeed indicator of the Doppler radar shows we've intruded into the core of a jet stream headwind. Far below, the North Atlantic is kicking up froth, but the engine is running without a murmur, and I don't hear any complaints from *Pole Cat*.

Scotland is an hour and twenty minutes astern when we sight a small fringe of Iceland's south coast peering out from under a cloud. It's time to start thinking about fuel. There will be tankers from England astride the Arctic Circle to the north of Keflavik. They call themselves *Amiable*.

"*Amiable* from *Julius Caesar*."

The first call makes a contact. Our aerial gas stations are ready to fill us up exactly as promised. In a few minutes we'll be swooping down on them.

While approaching Keflavik we spot an air-defense

fighter-interceptor making a head-on pass. I break left and Titus breaks right. The fighter goes streaking between us. We don't know exactly what that fellow had in mind. Maybe he was practicing. At any rate, there's little chance we could be incognito.

We join again and return to the fueling arrangements, chatting with *Amiable* as we approach our refuelers. Soon after passing Keflavik we ease slowly down toward the refueling altitude, closing fast on our tanker friends. Their airplanes are KB-50-Js, a hybrid species that carries a pair of jet engines as well as the four standard piston engines— an economical compromise with the jet age. Their radar- man vectors us in from astern and we soon catch sight of them. Those old airplanes may be hybrids but they look good from where we sit. As the fuel gauges drop lower, our affection for them increases.

The refueling job goes to Al Kucher. I missed the final practice sessions last week while flying my Pan Am sched- ule, and find it a luxury this time to let someone else take over the vigorous calisthenics. My exercise today is to run this expedition, and except for the lightweight chore of landing and taking off, it will be mostly mental, supervising what's going on and keeping track of the position, fuel, and navigation score. Right now we're one minute behind flight plan.

The fuel gauge reads a scant two thousand pounds, enough to return to Keflavik if the refueling apparatus fails to function. But if we should fail to hook up after making a few passes at the drogue, it would be imperative to turn the tankers back and refuel in a southerly direction, toward our refuge at Keflavik.

No need to worry about that. Kucher and Titus are razor-sharp, hitting the tanker drogues on the first pass. We start gulping the vital stuff, hanging onto the hoses until the fuel gauges show we're fat and full.

While fattening up we track due north, which will be

our route for the next few hours. The north coast of Iceland at the Arctic Circle passes underneath, its tan, treeless cliffs rearing out of the waters of Denmark Strait. After filling our tanks, we back off the hose and fly formation with the tankers for a few minutes. It's two hundred miles across Denmark Strait to Greenland. We'll stick with our refuelers for part of the distance and then top off our tanks. The extra gallons will allow a safe fuel reserve to return across Greenland to Thule if the next tanker rendezvous north of Greenland should misfire.

There are scattered-to-broken cloud layers all around but the visibility is good—so much so that the rugged mountains of Greenland come into view when more than a hundred miles distant. We go back on the hose, taking a last gulp of fuel before taking leave of our refuelers. We've left a big hunk of mileage behind us, and are starting anew. Before climbing to cruising altitude we catch a glimpse of the blue-black surface of the Greenland Sea, studded with a myriad of icebergs spawned by the glaciers that feed into Scoresby Sound. Jagged, snow-covered mountains rise from the icy ocean, forming a vista of stark desolation.

Julius Caesar crosses the 70th parallel of latitude at thirty-two thousand feet, heading due north. This marks the beginning of an eight-hundred-mile trek along the east coast of Greenland. But to the north of Scoresby Sound we're out of luck for scenery, not to mention the navigational luxury of flying the coastline. Layers of cloud mask the coastal mountains and Greenland's majestic, far-flung icecap. We lose touch with the earth, except for the fading radio chatter of the distant tanker men now returning toward Iceland.

I use the sun as my steering device, coordinated with the gyro compass. My work with the sun compass has by now become nimble. The practice session before reaching Iceland took the rust off my technique.

My steering job needs to be good. From Scoresby Sound it's eight hundred miles to the next radio checkpoint at Nord on the northeastern extremity of Greenland, little more than five hundred miles from the top of the world. But there is one discrepancy which jars my navigational composure. On the bow of the canopy slightly above eye level is a tiny standby compass. Its magnetic reading is 60 degrees. Flying due north where we are now it should read 35. The compass error is 25 degrees, as judged by the position of the sun. A 10 degree discrepancy might be expected in this area of Greenland. But 25 degrees of error don't add up, and the automatic navigation computers which we are testing are only as good as the heading information we feed them. This threat of a steering problem causes an extra flurry with the sun compass, and a double-check with my wing man in *Pole Cat*. Titus reveals his own standby compass is also reading high, or else we are on a wrong heading.

The celestial computer lent to me by one of SAC's most expert polar navigators, Dave Haney, gets a brisk workout as the bearing of the sun is checked and double-checked. I hold course as it dictates without fudging a single degree, but the obnoxious 60 degree reading of the magnetic compass stares back at me, challenging my belief in the integrity of the sun, and causing uncomfortable beads of perspiration to gather under the collar of my flying suit. I entertain visions of flying off into the ocean void that lies between Greenland and Spitzbergen. This would be navigational disgrace, among more disastrous consequences.

For instance, only two weeks ago I celebrated a boost in rank, and I don't relish becoming the shortest-term brigadier in Air Force history.

Instead of measuring relative bearings from the nose of the airplane, a technique which was so effective on my first polar journey, I'm using the more intricate aspects of the sun compass, adjusting latitude and hour angle in accordance with readings I've spun off Haney's hour-angle computer. This procedure, although it affords better accuracy, increases the possibility of a calamitous mistake, such as is being suggested by the misleading reading on the magnetic compass.

But the sun appears to be hanging just about where it should be in relation to the direction we're flying. We must press on. That sweat on the back of my neck will dry up when our track is finally verified by the radio direction finder. An hour from now it should pick up the radio beacon on the northeast tip of Greenland. Meanwhile, I bawl myself out for indulging in moments of doubt.

An hour passes, but the sea of milky cloud remains unbroken, merging all around into the brilliant blue of the sky. Finally I start tinkering with the radio compass. The northeastern tip of Greenland is not far distant. The radio direction-finder needle swings in circles a few minutes, then steadies and points over the nose at the Nord radio beacon. The last trace of doubt fades away. Meanwhile my earphones have picked up a faraway voice. Soon there are more voices—radio chatter between big airplanes of a tanker formation which calls itself Headburr.

As we close the gap the voices strengthen and finally they're loud and clear. I recognize the voice of Colonel Tara, who commands the tankers. They are from Langley Air Force Base in Virginia, and are northeast bound, crossing the icecap from the direction of Thule.

The tankers are approaching the beacon at Nord, where we're scheduled to rendezvous. There appears to be only one snag. Our friends from Virginia are flying formation on instruments in the clouds—which brings back recollections of the refueling difficulty in *Excalibur IV* east of Newfoundland during Shark Bait. We would all appreciate a little visibility for the hook-up.

I go on the air and carry on a brisk conversation with the distant refuelers. They are climbing in an attempt to top the clouds but, from where we sit at thirty-five thousand feet, the tops below us look pretty high for hybrid tankers. Finally the tanker commander reassures us they're between cloud layers to the north of Nord, with intermittent visibility.

We cross the 80th parallel of north latitude and become pips in the tankers' radar. The tankers track due north toward the Pole along the 18th meridian of west longitude, their radarman vectoring us in from astern. We cross the Nord radio beacon exactly on flight plan, and then bear down through the milky murk in close formation for the hook-up.

At twenty-four thousand feet between layers of thin stratus, we catch sight of the four tankers, then lose them intermittently in the wispy clouds. Coming up from behind we finally get a steady bead on our targets as we draw in close. Our probes slam home on the first pass. These troops are real pros.

We hang on and fill up, occasionally losing sight of the rest of the formation in the formless layers of broken cloud. In a few minutes, when full, we drop back to disconnect from the streaming hoses. The latitude now reads 83 degrees north, less than five hundred miles from the Pole. We'll stay together with our big friends for more than an hour, then get our final load of fuel at the top of the world before striking out down the meridian toward Fairbanks. This is one of our two flight plans—to stay with the tankers if there's a problem with the weather. Today it would be imprudent to do otherwise because the visibility tends to worsen as we fly north.

The other plan was to fly at normal cruising speed to the Pole, then orbit the top of the world while waiting for the tankers to catch up. However, I have some unforgettable memories of Shark Bait and decide to leave well enough alone. If the weather should be too cloudy at the Pole we would have difficulty rejoining our refuelers.

The tankers' auxiliary jet engines boost the ancient propeller airplanes along at a fair speed, but our fuel-glutted fighters find the pace uncomfortably slow. The

F-100s rear up to a high angle to maintain the awkward gait.

With jet tankers it would be a swift and easy pace. A single KC-135 tanker could have met us over Iceland, cruised along with us to a final refueling over the Pole, then left us to take care of other tanker business. But in 1959 the KC-135s were committed to bomber units and were rarely available for fighter exercise.

Our refueling companions maintain cautious separation from one another as we fly through the mists. Eventually the higher clouds break away and disappear altogether, exposing gray, unbroken clouds near the surface. The Arctic ice is totally enshrouded with mist.

My computer counts away the miles as we slip past each degree of north latitude. The sun hangs low over the left wing, inviting a reading with my sextant which shows we've strayed a few miles left of our chosen meridian, so we turn a few degrees to the right to pin down the magic spot that marks the top of the earth's axis.

It's time to get back on the hose for that last drink— the one for the road to Alaska. We go to work on a pair of fresh tankers, but this time *Excalibur V*'s probe nudges the edge of the drogue's conical receptacle, pushing it aside toward the cockpit canopy and causing the heavy drogue to graze the top within inches of my helmet. As we move further forward the heavy black hose slithers like a snake along the top of our fragile cage.

"That's great," growls Al Kucher, as he pulls away. We back off to try again and are soon hooked up. Meanwhile Bob Titus tells us his *Pole Cat* is filling up.

But the wayward drogue we've hooked onto turns out to be a dud. The stingy black hose refuses to yield a single drop. The diminished reading of the fuel gauge becomes unpleasant to behold.

A hollow voice from the tanker says, "Caesar lead, we've got no pressure."

Suddenly there is a more ominous malfunction. The troublesome hose starts a crack-the-whip motion. The long slender probe fastened to *Excalibur V*'s right wing bends crazily up and down with the violently whipping drogue to which it is attached. I have visions of the probe being ripped out of the wing, tearing a fatal hole in the fuel system and bringing our journey to an end at 90 degrees north latitude.

"That's great," Kucher sums up the situation again as he pulls back and disengages.

Disenchanted with this black, coiling monster, we move over to stab another drogue that streams from a hose behind the tanker's right wing. The fuel-gauge needle starts climbing and our sense of well-being climbs with it all the way to the "full" mark.

Still hooked up, we cross the top of the world and head south. I hear some spirited banter in my headphones as we take leave of this symbolic checkpoint at the North Pole. The fuel gauges have hit the full mark, so we pull away from our refuelers. We've won our independence again.

It seems crowded up here at the North Pole today, altogether different from my first trip eight years ago when I was alone in my P-51. The Arctic seemed a different place then—more formidable. It was a lonely, unshared thrill when I crossed the top of the world chasing that red ball in the sky.

For me it could never be like that again.

"So long, Julius Caesar," Colonel Tara bids us farewell.

"See you in the newspapers," someone chimes in.

The tankers stream graceful curving contrails as they bank left toward Greenland.

Moments ago it was the "evening" of August 7. Now it's the "morning" of the same day. We climb to thirty thousand feet and fly south along the 147th meridian.

Titus advises that the big, expensive navigation computer in his *Pole Cat* has run amuck. But we don't really need these computers today, except to test them for their future possibilities. At any rate, the less costly and less complicated computer in my airplane is still ticking away the miles. I've won my computer bet, and this could give the taxpayers a small victory over the big spenders.

One of my chores on this journey is to find out if the less intricate computer can do everything that needs to be done, providing I fill in for its small "capability" gaps with an occasional dose of low-key brainpower, an amount which would not degrade a fighter pilot's main function—that of weapons delivery. If the pilot's brain can be judiciously picked, we will come up with a navigational device which is less likely to break down, costs less, and occupies less space in the highly compressed black-box section of a fighter airplane where space is hard to find.

The line between too little automation and too much of it is very thin. One of my reasons for setting up this transpolar exercise was to help settle an argument about where this line should be drawn.

Back in the lab they call it a "human factors" study. To a test pilot it's a procedure to pin down what is essential and what is practical.

Up here in the far north we're dealing with equipment which presents navigational accuracy in terms of *miles*. Behind us, during six weeks in Italy we were testing a different kind of black box. We were looking for an answer to another, more productive question. Could a swift fighter-bomber navigate at low altitude in terms of *yards* instead of miles.

I was directed by the Office of the Secretary of Defense to test a British black box which was so precise it could guide an automobile through the streets of London in zero visibility pea-soup fog to a predetermined, totally obscured destination, and without bumping a curbstone. Certainly this kind of accuracy needed looking into for whatever else it could do.

I found it could do what we were looking for, and much more, during a series of flights over England. During my first bad-weather flight in an Italian G-91 jet fighter with this high-precision black box, I was astonished at the wide variety of bonanzas it could offer the driver of a speeding jet fighter if the right tactics and instrumentation were used. This was a big navigational breakthrough.

I felt like the hungry, frustrated prospector who accidentally stubbed his toe on a rich gold mine.

With the help of Charles S. "Buck" Weaver, director of foreign programs in the Pentagon, I had borrowed the Fiat G-91 from the Mutual Weapons Development Program, which was under the auspices of our Department of Defense and of NATO. This airplane, manufactured by Fiat in Turin, had been selected from a group of European-built fighters to be the standard NATO lightweight strike fighter.

During a foggy British November, with an expert from USAF's Eglin Air Force Proving Ground, Major Russ Crutchlow, doing most of the flying, the little black box scored many good points in the Italian fighter before we took the equipment to Italy for a further exercise at the Italian test center at Practica di Mare. Then, because we needed to include some American fighters in these Italian tests, I set up Operation Julius Caesar, and we flew our two F-100s across the Atlantic by way of the Azores and England to Rome, where they were temporarily equipped with this high-precision navigational gear.

We had some troubles at first, but they were soon shaken out, and the Italian exercise turned out to be a promising effort. Although we had hardly scratched the surface we could see the quality of the navigational "gold." It was rich.

But some black clouds were gathering on the horizon.

The first suggestion of trouble came after I visited a three-star general at SHAPE in Paris to tell him what we had been doing and that the results looked good. At that time we were donating some fighter airplanes to the Greeks and Turks, and I must have come close to convincing the general that the black box we had been testing would help them.

A couple of weeks later the roof of the Pentagon shook, and some bricks ricocheted off my skull. Our little black box was in deep trouble. In fact, it was so sick it had been quarantined by the United States government.

I've always thought leprosy was a grim disease, but this innocuous concoction of electronic wizardry had something worse. It was as politically unhealthy as a black box can be.

A distant cousin (which shall be anonymous) of this black box had become involved in an international argument about airway navigation aids for the airlines and other itinerant aircraft. This was a separate, unrelated matter, but it, too, would have unfortunate reverberations on the civil airways in the nineteen-sixties. The exclusion of *area-coverage** navigation techniques, which should have been

---

* The two principal short-range radio navigation systems available for common use are spoken of technically as (1) *point source,* and (2) *area coverage.*

Point-source systems incorporate the use of radio beacons which give a precise navigational fix when the aircraft receiver has arrived directly over the radio beacon transmitter, and which give radio bearings when flying between beacons. A good measure of precision fixing is also available to air vehicles within close range of the beacon transmitter if distance-measuring equipment has been added to the beacon's radio-bearing capability.

An *area-coverage* system can be envisioned as a "blanket" of radio signals covering an area of many thousands of square miles. High-precision navigational fixes are available anywhere, at any selected points within the area covered, to both surface and air vehicles.

Because each technique has its strong points and its deficiencies as well, there has been a pressing need for *both* systems to fulfill important civil and military navigational needs. *Point source* is a notably simple, quick-reference navaid, but *area coverage* unsnarls a number of navigational riddles that defy solution by *point source,* among them being its adaptability for establishing multiple-track airways to replace the present obsolete single-track airway network which is now inefficiently strung

made a vital supplement to the free world's VORTAC airway navigation network, would contribute to the eventual strangulation of America's air traffic control system during the airway rush hours. At New York's biggest airport it would not be uncommon to find more than twenty to thirty big jets lined up ahead of my Boeing 707, waiting for takeoff. On one occasion I would be number seventy-three in the line-up.

Although our fighter-bomber needs were totally unrelated to the civil-airways argument, we still could not escape the quarantine caused by the interference of industrial-military interests in matters that should have been, and should always be, decided by unprejudiced technical evaluations which serve to meet practical operating needs.

So we didn't get a proven and reliable black box which would certainly have found its way around the jungles of Southeast Asia with much the same precision that the fogbound automobile found its way around the streets of London.

High-precision navigation in fighter-bombers in the vital decade of the sixties would, therefore, be limited to excessive dependence on the human eyeball.

Washington's short-sighted approach to navigation problems would eventually take its toll in Vietnam. Not only would many people on our side needlessly die for lack of better guidance in our fighter-bombers, but also

---

between *point-source* airway beacons—one notable cause for defective air traffic control.

The more practical navigational experts have considered it would have been advantageous, and much less expensive in the long run, to have proceeded with the side-by-side development and use of *both* systems for wherever and whenever they would *both* become operationally necessary. However, in the crucial decision year of 1959 some short-sighted political maneuvering in the International Civil Aviation Organization (ICAO) banned *area coverage* as an officially recognized airway navigation aid until the next "decision year" of 1975. The imagined dollar savings of millions which prompted this regrettable action have paved the way for the waste of airway and military billions in the nineteen-sixties.

the weight of bombs dropped would often be many times the tonnage really needed if we could only have had the freedom to use some precise and versatile area-coverage electronic-guidance equipment.

Since 1960 there have been various superficial military evaluations of obsolescent or incomplete versions of the quarantined black box in Vietnam and elsewhere under United States supervision. But not even the best of concepts or equipment can survive a test where the accent is on the negative, when the equipment is tested for what it does *not* do, instead of what it *can* do.

On one occasion, in 1961, we almost lifted the quarantine with what would have been an inexpensive, practical evaluation of the controversial equipment. This tryout, which was to have been made at the Air Force Fighter Weapons Training Ground at Nellis Air Force Base, Nevada, would have shown the badly needed capabilities lying dormant in the black box. The price tag was a mere hundred thousand dollars for the illumination of the "can do" potential for all fighter-bomber test pilots to see. But we never got that test program. We fell short of one signature in the Pentagon.*

We almost penetrated that "bureaucratic thicket" which I quote from Admiral Rickover in an earlier chapter, but the paper work finally smothered us.

The admiral also had this to say about the Pentagon papermill:

"Lately I find myself thinking of the commission set up after the end of World War I by the Weimar Republic to study and report on the causes of Germany's defeat. The

---

* After years of delay it has been officially decided that high-precision area-coverage navigation has some potential use in military aircraft. An uncontroversial black box is now undergoing tests which, when further developed, will be useful in the nineteen-seventies. This delay, unfortunately, has cost us the navigational precision which has been badly needed, and which has been readily available, throughout the sixties.

commission found that a major cause of this defeat was the amount of paper work required of the armed forces. Toward the end they were literally buried in paper.

"I hope we will never have to appoint a similar commission."

So we lost the battle in the Pentagon. Nor am I free of blame. I pushed this project hard, but, I know now, I should have pushed harder.

Julius Caesar has been left dangling around the North Pole. It's time to accelerate the Old Roman down toward Alaska.

From the North Pole to Eielson Air Force Base near Fairbanks it's "downhill" for almost two thousand miles, including fourteen hundred miles of icy ocean, plus a few hundred miles of Alaskan mountains. But the complexities of the flight are behind us. Now it's mostly up to the engines.

But the engines are good ones, and they propel us past the coast of Alaska at Oligtuk at 2245. I hear someone make the usual pronouncement when any ocean is behind: "It's a piece of cake."

The clock says we're a couple of minutes late, so we shovel on more coal and pour thick contrails across the cloudless Alaskan sky. The mountains of the Brook Range slide behind.

It wouldn't be much trouble to push through to Japan, less than seven hours away. One more tanker hook-up over Fairbanks and another at the far end of the Aleutians would see us through, nonstop.

Because the final destination of these airplanes will be Japan, I made an effort to arrange for the tankers, but it didn't work out. So at thirty-five thousand feet over the winding Yukon the end of the line is in sight. Eielson is over the nose.

But there's trouble ahead. The airstrip has been invaded

by a big bull moose who has taken command of the middle of the runway. The Air Police are trying to coax him away.

We lose seven miles of altitude in a long dive and hustle across the base with the airspeed pushing the speed limit. The minute hand of the clock reads twenty-four, just as the crystal ball told us back in England. And the racket we make wins the argument for the Air Police. The king of the forest abdicates and hightails across the tundra, leaving the runway to Julius Caesar.

But the moose is luckier than I. He's going back to the primeval majesty of his wilderness. My destination is Washington—a place which, for me, seeking navigation precision, will become as barren as the Arctic tundra, and a place where crippling military-industrial politics will, in my view, lead to a significant degree of navigational impotence during the coming air action in Vietnam.

CHAPTER THIRTEEN

The Thorn and the Dagger

Bangkok on June 17, 1967, steams in the clammy heat of the summer monsoon. Towering gray rainclouds gather all around, thrusting their billowing white crests high above the muggy haze.

But all this stifling heat cannot stop the mind from thinking its own thoughts and mulling over memories and impressions of this part of the world gathered during many years of traveling around the circuit as a flying globe-trotter and a long-time Air Force adviser specializing in the problems of nuclear weapons delivery—memories and impressions stored away in a far corner of the brain to be taken out and reexamined on a day such as this.

Bangkok is a city with a multiple personality. It is a place which abounds with temples that remind one of more tranquil centuries. It is a bustling center of free commerce and an oasis along the jet airways, the hub of an airline network which stretches long distances in every direction except north, where the bristling underbelly of hostile Red China seals off the Western world.

The Thais are surrounded by danger, but it takes more than threatening weather or the warfare being waged all around to becloud their smiling good humor, a trait probably derived from generations of freedom from being kicked around by foreigners.

These people make Americans welcome because we're obviously not trying to possess them. Although we don't fit easily into the ancient Siamese scheme of things, these Orientals are aware we're not grinding any nineteenth-century colonial ax. Our chief aim, in spite of the wild chaos of our overinvolvement in Vietnam, is to help protect our less muscular friends from being possessed by anyone but themselves, if they really want it that way—the strength of such determination, we have discovered, is not easy to ascertain.

Our enemies call this "imperialism," but there are hundreds of millions of people around the perimeter of Red China who aren't eager to see the American style of "imperialism" pull back into a North American fortress. The vision of a nuclear-armed Peking dragon which fixes a hungry bloodshot eye on its easily digestible neighbors may be a nightmare even to the North Vietnamese and Ho Chi Minh himself.

So we've been involved in carnage and controversy, trying to contain an aggressive little nation until it, hopefully, sees the light. But holding it gently hasn't been easy. All the while we keep trying to remember that big fellows don't look good when they bash little guys over the head too energetically. Certainly, we can't split a little fellow all the way to the ankles with a nuclear cleaver even though he is tougher than we imagined.

It is a discomforting consequence that our preoccupation with North Vietnam has so strait-jacketed our international concern that we have little freedom of movement in considering much larger matters, such as the approaching nuclear confrontation with the Red Chinese, who threaten to be the most unpredictably dangerous of all antàgonists when they become armed with thermonuclear weapons.

The midday sun over Bangkok has pushed the mercury past a sultry ninety. The steamy atmosphere of the doldrums barely moves. But this day, so far, has been like any other. Nothing special has happened yet, not even the rain which threatens to dampen the afternoon.

However, the seventeenth day of June hasn't always been gently easygoing. Fourteen years ago, when the East Germans rose up and pelted rocks against the puppets who ruled them, it was a day that symbolized freedom in a place where even the word itself was a stranger. But that explosion was quickly muffled.

Today is doomed to be the anniversary of another eruption. But this one will be different. It will foreshadow a potful of trouble for the future of mankind. It will be a symbol of overwhelming force on the verge of getting out of control. It will resound for generations to come, but not in the cause of freedom.

June 17 also stirs a personal recollection. It is the thirty-fourth anniversary of my first assignment in the cockpit of an airliner—the night ride with Henry Boonstra across the mountains from Cheyenne to Salt Lake City.

Back in 1933 the airplane in the story was a Boeing 247. Today the aircraft I command is a Boeing 707. These years of international turbulence have pushed the technologists hard. Therefore our airliners fly four times faster and several times higher than before World War II. The 707 lifts thirty times the tonnage of the old 247, and today its passenger count is one hundred and fifty. It is a dramatic-looking flying machine which symbolizes the dynamism and wealth of the United States of America.

My assignment for June 17, 1967, is Pan Am's Flight Two, eastbound around the world. Our first stop after Bangkok will be Hong Kong. Today I'll be taking Flight Two as far as Tokyo, where we'll hand it over to the crew which is flying one day ahead of us.

We've been resting in Bangkok, which is one of our main stopovers along the airways. I've been coming here ever since 1960 for more than one reason. Sometimes I doff my airline cap and wander into the hinterland, carrying Air Force travel orders to odd-sounding places like Takhli, Udorn, Vientiane, and to that city full of trouble—Saigon.

Yesterday I was at Takhli, which is home base for the Air Force's 355th Tactical Fighter Wing. The commander there has been my friend and associate for many years, Colonel Bob Scott, assisted by one of the most aggressive of all combat aviators, Colonel Jack Broughton. I spent the day watching their F-105 troops, some of the most resolute professionals I've ever had the honor to mingle with, light their afterburners and blast off in the direction of Hanoi. *Excalibur VI*, which I had flown years before in the Nevada desert, was among those F-105s.

The scene is altogether different today. It will be business as usual, despite the fact that we'll be flying over the top of the most baffling of all wars. This is also the first war which can be flown over for the price of an airline ticket.

But the view from on high won't be authentic. The misery on the surface will not be visible from thirty-three thousand feet. The perspective will be deceptively serene except for the thunderheads which poke their threatening tops above our cruising level.

But there shouldn't be any MIGs or SAMs to hinder the progress of our world-circling flight. The sky, at least, is controlled by the guns of our side.

The route will take us across Thailand to Ubon, then across Laos and Vietnam to Danang. From Danang we'll bend around Red China's Hainan to Hong Kong. Hong

Kong will be two hours and twenty minutes out of Bangkok.

My crew totals nine—three males and six females. The men operate the front end of the Boeing. The girls are in the back. My copilot today is a veteran aviator from New York—Captain Charlie Grinnell. He took this trip to get acquainted with the route.

The Thailander in the tower clears us for takeoff. His voice is a brisk singsong. The tone is friendly. In spite of what our detractors say, we get along well with these Asians.

Three minutes after leaving the terminal the Boeing's big wheels slam up into their sockets. We don't fool around running up our jet engines. We just give them the gun, and they go.

A wall of clouds in the east doesn't look friendly, but our cockpit radar will sort the bumps out. Those nasty-looking white clusters on the radar threaten rough air, so we'll poke our nose into the soft spots in between. The cocktails back aft should hardly ripple.

Over Ubon we break out in the clear. The waters of the Mekong thread through the countryside ahead. On the far side of the big river is a stripling of a nation called Laos, pronounced "louse" by Americans. The French pronunciation is more kindly. They leave off the *s*. Here is a hunk of geography which is half friend, half foe.

The topography of that seemingly innocuous country has, by long study, been riveted into the back of my skull. Beyond the Mekong on the far side of this narrow strip of a nation winds a main supply artery of the enemy—the Ho Chi Minh Trail. The trail is fed by branches which come out of North Vietnam, reaching through the passes of a rugged spine of mountains along the border.

After many years in fighter cockpits, my thoughts are geared to what goes on inside the helmet of a fighter jockey flying close to the terrain. He does not find this to be a navigationally easy country. Landmarks are few and far between along Uncle Ho's supply line. The radar eyes of an airplane are little better than useless over this mishmash of mountains and jungle.

Moreover, this navigational vacuum applies to most of South Vietnam as well. From the air the villages look alike; the hills and valleys look alike. The vast spread of jungle and the open areas in between are full of navigational nothingness to a low-flying airplane. It's small wonder that our fighter-bombers sometimes scatter their weapons in the wrong places.

Which brings to mind some prickly memories of a failed project.

I think back a long way to Operation Julius Caesar and wonder how many lives and how much national wealth would have been saved if our fighter-bombers could have dissected their targets in Southeast Asia as precisely and dependably as that obscure little automobile threaded its way through the fogbound streets of London so many years ago.

I wonder if someone else could have done better than I and penetrated that bureaucratic jungle which defied all reason. Perhaps Dave Schilling could have. But Dave has been gone a very long time.

I recall a bullheaded "Don't confuse me with the facts" general. Every time we thought we had an opening into a better navigational future, the door was slammed shut. The obstructionist with the gift of gab was always there, plugging the dike against any new flow of intelligence.

I once had a Walter Mitty dream. I owned the United States Air Force. Four-star generals like LeMay and Disosway were running it. Other leaders with the style and intellect of Generals Joe Moore and Gordon Graham were moving up. But the bullhead, that head which spouted navigational nonsense, was being used for a bowling ball.

. . .

We're past the Ho Chi Minh Trail. Up ahead a mass of gigantic monsoon clouds obstruct the flight path to Danang. The cockpit radar is full of menacing-looking white clumps which stretch a long way south. We must detour toward the north or take a beating.

We thread our way between the DMZ and Danang, and break into the clear with the Benhai River down below on the left. Here is the 17th parallel of north latitude—the magic number which splits the two Vietnams.

The visibility to the north is unlimited. Only the earth's curvature hides the Russian weapons proving ground that surrounds Hanoi and Haiphong.

A ribbon of sand separates the dark green of the jungle from the deep blue of the South China Sea. But this is no easygoing bathing beach. There's no frolicking here. The thickets alongside the beach could be full of trouble.

The beaches slide past the tail of the 707. Vietnam, the toughest of all thorns in Uncle Sam's hide, is behind.

This may be a mere thorn in our side, but today is June 17, 1967, and we Americans are about to feel the first searching prick of a dagger, which is aiming for the heart.

The coast of China comes to view a long way out. A gentle summery haze softens the coastline and hides the grim miseries of the teeming humanity beyond. Even Macao looks immaculate from a distance, and the white masonry of Hong Kong glistens in the sparkling sunshine against its spectacular setting of green mountains and azure-blue harbor.

We drop low across the roofs of Kowloon and bend around toward Kowloon Bay for a landing on runway 13. A thirty-mile-an-hour crosswind with a few knots on the tail adds spice to the approach.

It sometimes gets spicy in the streets of Hong Kong, too. But we only read about it in the newspapers. Ninety minutes at the airport can't show anyone the seamy side of Asia.

We take leave through Lyemun Gap and head out toward Checkpoint Whiskey. The next stop will be Tokyo, three hours and twenty minutes to the northeast.

The China coast still looks placidly serene in the deepening haze. The red ball of the sun lowers itself gracefully in the west-northwest.

But out beyond that coastline, out of sight and sound, in the hinterland beyond the Gobi, almost in line with that red ball in the sky, the scene has been less than tranquil.

Three megatons of thermonuclear fury have exploded across the desert of Takla Makan.

Postscript

Those years in the "think factory" which followed the Arctic adventure have not been comforting. Among other things, one learns how easy it can be, in a free society such as ours, to plant catastrophic weapons where they can do the most harm. And because the Chinese, of all people, have always made the best kind of firecrackers, it is not unreasonable to think of them also as expert manufacturers and purveyors of nuclear weapons.

Therefore, in Tokyo on the morning of June 18, when I woke up to read the bleak headlines of yesterday's happening, I felt an extra twinge of concern for the safety of my own country.

For the Japanese, this Red Chinese achievement was a disturbing reminder of Hiroshima and Nagasaki, the first urban victims of nuclear energy on a rampage. And if that weren't enough, an old adversary now toting atoms loomed menacingly on the horizon, guided by a deified zealot in Peking who (at least to some of us who have worked with nuclear weapons) suggest that Adolf Hitler, at the peak of his mania, was a minor madman.

We Americans, on the other hand, haven't yet felt the blast of the exploding atom, and we console ourselves that we're separated from Peking by the widest of all oceans. Although our leaders have taken anxious note of the big Chinese test, the public reaction to the explosion of June 17 in this most affluent of all nations was strikingly nonchalant. Being tragically uninformed and uninterested in the process of digging into unpleasant nuclear facts, most Americans can't begin to imagine what the big Chinese dagger could really mean to us.

New York's leading newspaper limited its portentous headline of June 18 to a sedate two columns. Its writers were possibly hoping against hope that Mao Tse-tung would soon be replaced by someone less fanatical. Meanwhile, the popular notion is that, despite the absence of nuclear controls with respect to China, our strategic forces will still keep aggressors at arm's length until we're much closer to the end of this bloodiest of all centuries when, hopefully, reason may prevail.

Our key national policy of deterrence has worked well with the Soviets. When the Russians stared down the nuclear gun barrel in October of 1962 and didn't like the looks of it, they turned their missile ships around and went home. At that moment it was revealed that the United States of America and the U.S.S.R. could live on the same planet together, provided, of course, that we're careful not to soften too much, and that the Russian and American gunners in and around Berlin, the Middle East, and various other places exercise restraint.

Now that the technocrats are gaining more influence in

Russia, we occasionally see a hopeful sign for the future. As a small example, on June 17, while the Chinese were splitting their atoms over Takla Makan, the premier of the U.S.S.R., Alexsei N. Kosygin, felt mellow enough to leave his limousine and take an informally brisk walk among Americans up Third Avenue in New York City, of all places. In fact, he made it all the way from 55th to 67th Street without being held up for even so much as an autograph.

Nor is there any reason to believe that the Russians are any happier about the new Chinese thermonuclear weapons than we are. They're certainly not unaware of their thousands of miles of common border with a nation which bulges with nearly a billion industrious people. On June 18, in the wake of the Chinese thermonuclear test, a Muscovite man on the street expressed his reaction to a visiting reporter of the New York Times. "Good Lord," he said. "What's going to happen to us? They are madmen."

And so they may be, but they could be mad like a fox.

To this ex-inmate of a "think factory" the official response of the Pentagon to the Chinese explosion of June 17 seemed altogether too comforting. The Joint Chiefs soothingly announced there would be no threat to American cities until the Chinese have created a large force of intercontinental ballistic missiles (ICBMs).

But can we Americans afford to be so easily lulled into a state of complacent apathy? Should we not start asking some questions?

Are we not mistaken in ranking airplanes and ICBMs as the maximum menace to our own free society, where just about anything can penetrate?

Are we not too steeped in the lore fostered by the lobby of our aviation and space complex? Are we not too smugly secure because of our own orderly skyborne techniques which are the best means we have for penetrating the closed societies of our enemies?

Moreover, considering the abnormalities of the Red Chinese psyche, might it not be prudent to take another look at our policy called deterrence which, since our 1962 confrontation with the Russians, has taken on an aura of infallibility? Is it really true that the Red Chinese will fall in line as the Soviets did when they stare down that nuclear gun barrel? Are they really afraid of massive retaliation?

What do the Red Chinese think about our deterrence concept? Could it not easily come within the realms of probability that their zealous leadership, which is the kind of guidance the Chinese people themselves are likely to accept longer than we like to contemplate, will be willing in their extreme ambition, to take calculated risks with their nuclear arms? Could they not be emboldened by the omnipotence of a seething billion population which could take the shock of a nuclear exchange and still leave hundreds of millions of unscathed Chinese remaining in the remote countryside, people who would scarcely be aware that anything catastrophic had happened?

Moreover, we and the French have had plenty of experience with Asians who think the next world will be a better place to live in than this one.

Still, on the other hand, it is reasonable to say that even an irrational leader would not strike out with nuclear fury until he possessed all the weapons he needed, together with the means for their delivery. Certainly, an indecisive number of intercontinental ballistic missiles would not only fail to achieve a strategic victory, it would also invite instant retaliation.

But will Red China be likely to rely on the expensive and elaborate ICBM? It would take a long time and great expense to create a defensive force.

Therefore, is it not logical they may seek a quicker, cheaper, and safer method to achieve decisive results—a stealthy method which is more likely to confuse us and con-

sequently be less certain to invite massive retaliation? Certainly, it's no secret there are less conventional and more effective means of nuclear delivery than any intercontinental ballistic missile.

We need to face the fact that ultra-modern military delivery techniques do not present the most menacing nuclear problem. Surely the easiest to deliver, toughest to combat, most accurate, and for selective targeting the most devastatingly effective of all explosive weapons systems is the ground transported thermonuclear bomb, which in its smaller sizes can be borne to its target in the most uncomplicated of all delivery capsules—a suitcase!

Certainly any ground vehicle would be more deadly accurate than any airplane, or any intercontinental missile when conveying a furtive device to the exact location where it could do the most harm. Nor is there any military technique for countering small, hidden weapons which explode with the force of thousands, in fact millions, of tons of TNT. Furthermore, it would be difficult and time-consuming to determine precisely whom to retaliate against.

Although the more rigid among American military minds argue otherwise, anyone who has been around knows that a significant number of omnipotent weapons could be stealthily planted at strategic locations with very little trouble at all. Understandably this ultra-simple weapons delivery technique is an unpopular concept at the Pentagon because it degrades the Joint Chiefs' unbending theory that a vast deployment of anti-missile missiles is the best protection against the thermonuclear threat.

On the other hand, there are plenty of military and "think factory" people who are uneasy about this costly anti-missile concept. They are convinced it is undependable and a mere defensive palliative, and that there is no effective defense against any determined attack with a large multiplicity of thermonuclear weapons. There are just too many valid delivery techniques.

For example, in our scheme of things, is there any easier way to deliver a small nuclear package than, for instance, by motor vehicle?

And we have one hundred million of these.

Furthermore, we have a growing multitude of destructive civilians.

Are the Red Chinese going to be blind to the advantages they could derive from peddling their small-size thermonuclear weapons to civilian trouble-makers (bearing in mind the other, more affluent nuclear nations could hardly be imagined rocking the nuclear boat by so doing)? Here is a route to chaos and conquest which would fail to invite any massive retaliation at all.

As world affairs are shaping up, any tightly organized, destruction motivated group of nuclear-armed civilians could, in the not-too-distant future, become much more of a menace than the strait-laced military threat where the restraints are severe and retaliation certain.

In the final analysis, what is a reliable and realistic defense against these proliferating weapons? Is there any authentic protection, except international control, to replace the dwindling concept of deterrence with respect to Red China and to check the growing civilian threat—bearing in mind that the Russians, too, are aware of their own vulnerability as a next-door neighbor of the Chinese?

What are the other options, considering that time is running out on the possibilities for control?

Shall we hide behind a Maginot Line which bristles with complex defensive devices in a futile effort to ward off every enemy delivery technique that comes along, at a cost of too many billions and at the risk of weakening vital military programs?

Or shall we divert most of those billions which are likely

to be earmarked for "defensive palliatives," and spend them instead to renew our environment and our cities, and to take care of other national priorities, so that our more destructive citizens can find little excuse for helping engineer and execute their own "urban renewal" program with devastating explosives?

Meanwhile, the question of control of totally unrestrained and potentially footloose thermonuclear weapons needs to be given higher priority and deeper concern than it is now getting, and without delay.

Every tick of the clock brings the danger closer.

Time *is* on their *side*.

Time, until weapons control is achieved, will be our enemy.

INDEX